SAVING LIVES WHILE

FIGHTING FOR MINE

STORIES TO EMPOWER WOMEN TO WIN

This book was compiled by visionary:

International Best-Selling Author, Ayanna Mills Gallow

Co-Authors: Alison Brown, Chany Rosengarten, Charmane West,

Dr. Charmaine Gentles, Dr. Keesha Karriem, Jacinta Wolff, Lisa Campbell,

Lisa Lamazzi, Martha King, Tiffani Teachey, and TrevisMichelle Mallord

---

Connect with Alison
simplyalisonbrown.com

DISCLAIMER

Disclaimer: Any information, characters, and events within the compilation of stories or other related and linked materials are the sole opinion of each individual author and are for entertainment use only. The views expressed have no relation to those of any academic, hospital, office practice, or corporate institutions with which the authors are affiliated. Neither the lead author, nor co-authors, are dispensing medical or legal advice and do not intend any of this information to be used for self-diagnosis, treatment, or legal strategy. Never disregard professional medical or legal advice or delay in seeking it because of something you have read in this book or in any related and linked materials.

If you think you may have a medical emergency, call your doctor or emergency room immediately. To the maximum extent permitted by law, the author, related entities, and the publisher disclaim all responsibility and liability to any person, arising directly or indirectly from any person taking or not acting based on the information provided.

TABLE OF CONTENTS

ACKNOWLEDGMENTS

I give honor to God from whom all my blessings flow. To each author who shared their story to contribute to such an ambitious and worthy project: I am in awe of your accomplishments, determination, and humility. Your stories are powerful beyond measure, and I have no doubt that they will impact many women to find the courage to embrace their pain and overcome their shame.

To Dr. Janell Jones: My eternal gratitude for your far-reaching vision, inspirational leadership, and endless encouragement.

To our editor, Tamika Sims: Thank you for helping us bring clarity and polishing our testimonies so that we may share them with the world.

Finally, a heartfelt thanks to our special loved ones, near and far, who are our biggest cheerleaders and tireless supporters in all our endeavors. Your support has contributed to our fight for survival and ultimately saved our lives.

DEDICATION

This book is dedicated to anyone who experienced life's painful situations that resulted in feelings of hopelessness and shame. We want you to know that it is normal to deal with hard times, but you were created to win and live a satisfying life.

"For I know the plans I have for you," says the Lord.
"They are plans for good and not for disaster, to give you a future and a hope."

Jeremiah 29:11 NLT

This book is also dedicated to anyone keeping secrets to avoid embarrassment or judgment from others. God wants your life to be whole and complete. He blessed you with family, friends, counselors, and coaches. Even if you don't want to talk to those you know, then we encourage you to seek help so that you can heal and have success on the inside and the outside.

We pray that our stories will provide you with hope so that you can bounce back and be better than before.

"For I reckon that the sufferings of this present time are not worthy to be
compared with the glory which shall be revealed in us."

Romans 8:18 KJV

FOREWORD

Dr. Janell Jones

What comes to your mind when you hear the word hero? Usually, when we think of heroes, we think of a person with a cape on going into a burning building saving the damsel in distress. The damsel is usually a young, beautiful, single woman who is in awe by the hero rescuing her. Most of the time you see the beginning of their story, the middle, and then they live happily ever after. What if I introduced new heroes to you? A group of women who wake up every day to save others- but in the background, they had to make the tough decision of saving themselves.

According to *Merriam-Webster*, a hero is defined as "a person who is admired for great or brave acts or fine qualities." One definition of hero surprised me: the chief male character in a story, play, or movie. I'll be the first to say, I love our men. They are needed and important... so I will never discredit them. If anything, I would simply ask Webster to redefine the word *hero*, as you'll learn these women have had tremendous acts of bravery. They overcame situations many people wouldn't have survived, and still found the courage to help others. They could've remained stuck in their pain, but they decided to share their stories to transform the lives of many women who are in similar categories.

Now, let me take some time to brag about the visionary author, Ayanna Gallow. I first met Ayanna on a three-city book tour in 2019. The first thing I noticed about Ayanna was her contagious and inviting smile. I thought, "Wow! This is someone with great energy." She seemed like she was always happy. During the tour, Ayanna shared her story about her childhood trauma. I couldn't believe the words coming out of her mouth; talk about judging a book by its cover. Ayanna didn't look like what she went through. This sharp-minded, well-dressed, confident woman is what I saw speaking on the stage. I was in disbelief to learn about what she went through and still able to have a smile on her face and exude passionate energy.

As time went on, Ayanna and I started working and collaborating on different projects. Learning more about Ayanna, I saw she was excellent at helping people share their stories. Not those fluffy stories that don't have meaning, but those unforgotten, deep-rooted, and ground-breaking stories. These are the stories that many people suffer in silence and have created a chokehold on their lives.

Ayanna coached them through telling their stories, healing while they're writing, and removing their shame. She guides them to take their stories to transform not only the lives of others but their own. She teaches them how to be business owners, coaches, course creators, and authors.

I also had the opportunity to hear the stories of the 11 heroes in this book. When I heard their stories, I was flabbergasted. I couldn't believe how these women had survived such difficult circumstances and still had the energy to be on the frontlines to save other people. These women made the choice to wake up every day to go to work, serve other people, go back home, and do it all again. Please don't take it lightly that these women shared their stories; it wasn't easy. However, they were able to be vulnerable in hopes they could help others going through.

I know when you read these heroes' stories, they will resonate. Somehow, someway, you'll be able to pinpoint yourself or someone else through their pain. But this book doesn't only offer you stories of how these heroes overcame. It provides you with a play-by-play of how they transformed their lives in order to help other women win.

You see these heroes aren't damsels in distress or victims. In fact, when deciding to save themselves they had to think about their children, education, relationship, finances, mindset, health, motherhood, and employment. What if these women decided to quit? What if they decided to not push through?

What if they would have said, "My story isn't important" or "Who would want to read my story?" You will now get to know their journeys to empower you to win... in every aspect of your life. So instead of these ladies waiting for the superhero to come and rescue them, they decided to put on a cape of their very own.

Get ready for this amazing journey!

Dr. Janell Jones

INTRODUCTION

Ayanna Mills Gallow, MBA

What if I told you that your present problem will bring you healing and happiness later? Would you stay and fight? Or, would you give up because your pain feels unbearable?

My name is Ayanna Mills Gallow and my past pain brought me to my purpose, which is why I am the visionary author of *"Saving Lives While Fighting for Mine: Stories to Empower Women to Win."* My vision for this book is to provide transformational non-fiction stories, written by women once powerless and now are powerful.

The purpose of this book is to discuss the authors' success following low self-esteem, financial trouble, unfair discrimination, and sexual trauma- in order to empower other women. Through the personal stories shared, I hope this book will prevent young women from making common mistakes, motivate women in the middle of a mess, and guide all women to triumph over trauma.

Survival of The Fittest

According to the CDC, women are more likely to experience child sexual abuse and sexual assault. In addition, 5 of every 10 women (or 50%) experience at least one trauma in their lives. Thus, it was no surprise to me when I learned that 10 of every 100 women (or 10%) develop PTSD sometime in their lives compared with about 4 of every 100 men (or 4%). Therefore, from childhood to adulthood, women deal with trauma.

Although so many women face trauma, they are often afraid to discuss their pain with others. They conceal their pain as a result of shame, which leads to negative emotions. They suffer in silence and walk around with a mask by pretending that everything is okay. I know this well because I wore that mask for a long time. Allow me to introduce the origin of this book, my transformation, and the purpose of *Saving Lives While Fighting for Mine: Stories to Empower Women to Win.*

House of Pain

I am amongst the 1% of people conceived in rape. My mother's stepfather raped her, which resulted in my birth. I was born six weeks after my mother's 13th birthday. If you think that sounds bad, then let me add to that by saying that my grandmother allowed her rapist husband to remain in the home and I grew up in the house with both of them. Traumatic, I know.

That experience caused me to be silent regarding my feelings. I chose silence because I thought I was unwanted. Therefore, I needed to be seen and not heard, and avoid all confrontation to prevent any further noise going on around me. As a result of the dysfunction from my childhood, I suffered internal pain and I suffered alone.

My pain came from feeling unwanted because I didn't have a normal family. I was embarrassed by my father/step-grandfather. I had to watch him succumb to cirrhosis of the liver caused by excessive drinking from guilt. I was sad for my grandmother. I had no idea why she let my father, who was her husband, remain in the home after he raped my mother/her daughter.

I was also scared for my mother because I feared her survival due to the painful look she displayed every time others would react negatively after learning we were only 13 years apart. Most painfully, I was devastated for myself because I could never change the fact that the blood running through my body came from a rapist.

For me to overcome the emotions of childhood trauma and transform to lead a prosperous life, I had to start with recognizing that I cannot change the past, who was wrong, or who was at fault; I had to experience a mindset shift.

I also grew in my relationship with the Lord and learned that He had and still has an awesome plan for my life. This helped me to stop thinking I was the child of a rapist. I focused on being a child of God first, and the child of a rape survivor second. If you are wondering, "how does one live with joy after being conceived in rape?" The answer to that is, they own who they are and are grateful to be a part of the 1% of babies "born" after conceived in rape versus the many aborted.

Even when I felt overwhelmed with negative emotions, I had to keep going because of my mother. Despite her pain, she took care of me and protected me and I wanted to do the same for her by not causing her any more pain. I also spent time in therapy and began sharing my story to give others hope and motivation.

In 2019, I wrote and published a book titled, ***God & Hip Hop: A 21 Day Biblical Devotional Inspired by Hip Hop***. In this devotional, I revealed the story of my birth. It shocked many people to learn that I suffered in silence. It especially surprised those I've known for over 30 years because I have an education, professional career, and an overall successful life. Hence, they had no idea I was wearing the mask of happiness on my face.

After the book was released, people began confiding in me about their struggles because they felt better after hearing mine. That's when I knew I had to do more. I thought if one story could have a positive effect on others, plus give me peace from sharing it; then how many people can a book of multiple transformational stories impact? Therefore, I began compiling transformational non-fiction stories and you are about to embark on my latest one.

The BluePrint

In *Saving Lives While Fighting for Mine: Stories to Empower Women to Win*, we want you to win in your finances, win in your minds, and win in every aspect of life. You are about to read 11 amazing stories on Equality Empowerment, Self-Worth Empowerment, Financial Empowerment, and Sexual Trauma Survivors Empowerment. I am excited about the final story that you will read because it was written by the 13-year-old teenager that I was blessed to be born to. I am happy that my mother found her healing and that she feels free to tell it. Therefore, to answer the question I posed at the beginning of this introduction; **Yes, your greatest pain can bring you healing and happiness later!**

EQUALITY EMPOWERMENT

"I ask no favor for my sex.
All I ask of our brethren is that they take their feet off our necks."

Ruth Bader Ginsburg

THE INEQUITIES IN PROFESSIONAL ADVANCEMENT FOR MINORITY NURSES

Charmaine Gentles, DNP, ANP

Healthcare institutions underrepresentation of minorities in leadership roles in the United States is concerning (Rosella, Regan-Kubinski, Albrecht, 1994). Many organizations such as the Institute of Medicine (IOM), and American Nurses Association (ANA) have highlighted the urgency to address this issue. These organizations cited that not having diverse leadership in healthcare will have substantial harmful effects on health care delivery and outcomes (IOM, Smedley et al., 2017 Paradies et al., 2015).

The urgency to increase minority leadership roles in healthcare is needed more now than before to reflect the diverse population and care needed. Diverse leaders are capable of mirroring and understanding the various cultures to meet the health care needs in a changing environment in the 21st century. Ultimately, trust is the foundation of patient-centered care. Trust is promoted when healthcare professionals provide care to the same cultures across the continuum.

My objective for writing this chapter is to bring awareness of the challenges faced by minorities, especially black women in healthcare. Obtaining leadership and influential opportunities in healthcare organizations is limited. In general, having conversations regarding diversity and racism is not easily entertained in an atmosphere where the majority of the senior leaders in authority are non-minorities.

Having lived the experiences as a minority in healthcare from nursing school to where I am today, has provided me with a substantial amount of information to determine a healthy healthcare working environment. I will describe personal encounters and how institutional racism has affected minorities as well as provide strategies that can help leaders support minority practitioners in obtaining leadership and executive roles in healthcare.

Fortunately, as referenced by Sally Field, (1946), "I never addressed myself to any image anybody has of me. That's like fighting with ghosts." If I did, I would not be able to write this chapter at this time. As a minority woman and a nurse leader, I am confident in who I am and strong enough not to allow anyone to undermine my sense of self. Having a Doctor of Nursing Practice degree, along with the understanding, extensive clinical experience, and the challenges faced throughout my years as a practicing clinician, I am qualified to address the many issues on leadership opportunities in nursing as it pertains to race and ethnicity.

Understanding the pathway, experiences, and challenges encountered along my journey is crucial. I chose nursing as a profession because of the need I have to improve population health and the love for my patients. My nursing career started as a bedside nurse for many years then transitioned to a nurse practitioner and program manager for a surgery specialty program in a large healthcare institution accounting to 24 years of practice. Based on the afore-mentioned it is relatively easy for me to recognize healthcare institutions' patterns of behaviors; diversity or lack thereof, leadership opportunities, and advancements for minority nurses.

In 2014, it was reported that 80% of healthcare workers were women, however only 43% represented at the executive level. In 2015, in another report, minorities held only 11% of the executive leadership positions in US hospitals. This is largely related to the underrepresentation of women and minority leaders in healthcare organizations for various reasons including exclusion, invalidation, assumptions, institutional neglect, and differential treatment. This resulted in psychological stress among minorities, negatively impacting clinical output, morale, and patient care. The psychological burden and consequences of inequality are debilitating.

Most minority healthcare professionals are left with feelings of despair, increased stress, feelings of anxiety, and social isolation when issues of racial discrimination are addressed. There are many occasions where minorities' psychological and emotional well-being were compromised to accommodate others. Heightened anxiety and emotional trauma results from working in such an environment. This kind of marginalization and minimization negatively impact the morale and psyche of the minority.

I am grateful that many of my colleagues who recognized these disparities constantly encouraged me to stay strong. Some saw the inequality however, they were afraid to speak up because they didn't want to lose their job. A common theme among executive management in healthcare is "we are here to help you." But are they really? Quite commonly, when race becomes a topic of discussion, it heightens awareness, however, it is quickly denounced, and the negativity is then projected onto the person who is being discriminated against.

Perception vs. Reality

Labels such as "trouble-maker, insubordinate" are assigned, and fearing for disciplinary actions, the individual subsequently becomes silent. Unbelievably, I too have previously encountered subtle threats jeopardizing my job if I continue to speak up. Over the years, I learned that many minority workers have similarly felt threatened by their superiors but were afraid to report it.

Why is this type of behavior welcomed in a healthcare climate? Isn't this ironic? We are fighting to save all of our patients' lives while fighting for our own existence. Minorities are constantly reminded that they will not be able to advance into leadership roles as the organizations don't encourage "such behaviors." The fear of job security, making the situation worse, the belief that nothing will be done, and labeled as being aggressive, leaves the psychological, physiological, and behavioral burden on minorities.

Who is advocating for minorities?

Many minorities in healthcare voiced their opinions that they believed human resources takes sides with the administrative and organizational leadership with regards to complaints of racial injustice rather than with them. Who is advocating for minorities at this point? Who can they trust? Where is the diversity and inclusion initiative in these major healthcare facilities? Many don't have a diversity officer. An individual perception can severely impact the way he/she functions in any given environment, including healthcare organizations. Non-verbal communication such as body language and behaviors in its most subtle form can be easily recognized by minorities due to differences.

This level of dissonance creates poor wellbeing, loss of confidence, humiliation, low morale, weakens the immune system creating physical illnesses, and poor work performance requiring time off from work. Ultimately, the organization loses highly motivated minorities and acquires those who are less driven and less motivated.

The experiences of discrimination, unequal career opportunities, and marginalization among ethnic minority nurses are well published in the literature (Iheduru-Anderson, 2019). This visible factor impairs our capabilities to succeed in the healthcare environment. Minorities' points of view are often disregarded, overlooked and expressed bias are often noted as being too sensitive.

For many minorities, potential leadership opportunities are underrepresented by race and not by abilities and qualifications. In moments like this, validation of cultural diversity in hire becomes apparent. There were people who I admired and respected in the healthcare profession who pretended to be supportive but covertly realized they are not.

There are many qualified minority nurses who have not been afforded leadership opportunities despite their advanced degrees and contributions. What is most difficult is "hearing how great you are, how much they "appreciate the work you've been doing," how much "you're respected among your peers." Despite all of this, they are not afforded an opportunity to be seated in executive leadership positions. Where is the motivation for minority female nurses beyond their desire to deliver excellence in healthcare, and deliver that experience to the betterment of their patients and institutions?

All the while seeing their white counterparts often with less clinical expertise, education, and training are afforded executive leadership roles and then the more experienced and qualified minorities are requested to train them. This is hurtful, to say the least. Do they realize the negative impact this has on the individual's well-being or is it that they do know, and don't care? For most, it is a constant struggle to achieve executive leadership opportunities in such an environment where they have dedicated their entire nursing career. However, I hope that my advancement from Nurse to Nurse Leader will inspire other minority nurses.

Professional Advancement

As a nurse practitioner, I provide direct patient care to a specialized group of patients as well as serve as the program manager. I work with a wonderful group of surgeons and administrators who are motivating and culturally sensitive. Daily, I ensure patient and staff safety are maintained, optimize patient experiences and outcomes. Applying the construct of emotional intelligence, I realized that more work is needed to improve patient care and patient outcomes and so, I decided to undergo the Doctor of Nursing Practice Degree (DNP) particularly to obtain expertise in evaluating care delivery processes, to ensure safety and quality care, to identify healthcare organizational issues and to facilitate changes in healthcare.

Through this education and training, I gained the knowledge to strengthen my leadership and collaborative skills. I exemplified this through the development of specific patient and nursing education, safety strategies, and implemented the best-practices, supported by the best available evidence for patients undergoing metabolic and bariatric surgery across many programs in the health system. Many often comment on my unique approach and vision to patient safety and quality improvement efforts to promote excellence in clinical practice. I am proficient in the necessary skills, have the clinical expertise that brought about effective changes both locally and nationally as well as national recognition for the organization for which I work. Therefore, Nurse leadership for minorities may be challenging, but it is still possible. These are the keys that I attribute to my success:

1. **Education & Training:** I transformed from a RN with an associate degree to a RN with a doctorate in Nursing (DNP) as well as a registered Nurse First Assistant (RNFA). Achieving my DNP and RNFA education and training has allowed me to function at a higher level as a minority woman in healthcare and in surgery.

2. **Evaluate and Translate Evidence-Based Research into Clinical Practice:** I am able to integrate available evidence, individual preferences and values of the population of patients served in the clinical setting. I evaluate research articles, develop in-services, teach nurses, and other healthcare providers how to provide care to a unique population of patients.

3. **Interprofessional Collaboration & Partnership**: I partnered with peers and physicians committing to interact constructively in redesigning the way we provided care to a unique population of patients to accomplish established goals and outcomes. I am a published author and have co-authored many peer-review healthcare journal articles and book chapters.

4. **Displaying Leadership**: As a resonant leader, I encourage my colleagues and team members to feel comfortable and connected to each other. I encourage others to be innovative, visionary and take risks. I'm empathetic to others' feelings and understand their point of view.

5. **Mentoring**: I progressed through the level of novice to an expert during my development. Having the requisite, knowledge, education, training, skills, and a unique level of clinical expertise I am able to provide mentorship to new nurses in the field and mentor others in evidence-based practice methods.

6. **Support**: Provide support through listening, empathy, and compassion.

7. **Professional Speaking and Networking:** I have been a local and national speaker promoting patient safety and improvement strategies in an exemplary bariatric program.

8. **Diligence:** With such exemplary work, I am a product of what I have achieved despite the challenges encountered as a minority woman in healthcare.

9. **Mindset:** Believe in yourself and establish credibility.

10. **Build A Bridge Among Healthcare Professionals**: Respect other team members knowledge and expertise.

11. **Emotional Intelligence**: Accurately assess your leaders' behaviors and the institution's emotional environment.

Institutional Racism

The realities of racial biases and discrimination in healthcare have always been disregarded and dismissed. It is evident that we have the requisites, the appropriate competencies, education, and training to obtain leadership advancement. Minorities are here to stay, and it makes no sense to marginalize and disregard us, we are not going anywhere.

Several written policies addressing racism are implemented in the healthcare working environment. However, one thing is for certain, employees abide by its construct. Are senior leaders abiding by these same principles? If so, why are there so many reports of minority nurses in healthcare in fear of losing their jobs if they speak up? Could it be that senior executive leaders are not aware of what is happening at the lower level? Minorities lack the support they need. Support must be visible by senior management to build trust among minorities so that they are free to discuss inequality in leadership roles. Senior leaders must educate themselves to recognize their own prejudices to combat subtle and unspoken racism.

They must be available to have constructive interracial conversations to minimize bias. They must make a personal commitment to identify and encourage minorities to report subtle aspects of racism in the healthcare environment. This will establish a diverse leadership in the workforce. Healthcare leaders should be more cognizant, remove the mask, and do more to promote an inclusive working environment for minorities if they are truly committed to establishing a diverse environment. Regarding minority healthcare professionals, stay steadfast in your dreams and goals, the system is the problem, not you.

References.

1. *Rosella JD, Regan-Kubinski MJ, Albrecht SA. The need for multicultural diversity among health professionals. Nurs Health Care. 1994;15(5):242-246.*

2. *Institute of Medicine. (1994). Balancing the scale of opportunity: Ensuring racial and ethnic diversity in the health professions. Washington, D/C; The National Academies Press. https:??doi.org/10.17226/4418*

3. *Smiley, RA, Laurer, P. Bienemy C, eta al. (2017). The National Nursing workforce survey. Journal of Nursing Regulatory. 2018; 9(3Ssuppl: S1-S28.*

FROM DISCRIMINATION TO DOCTORATE DEGREE

Dr. Keesha L. Karriem

I have three strikes against me. I am Black, I am a Woman and I am a Muslim. Unfortunately, I was a prime target for job discrimination. No matter how hard I worked or how much education I possessed; I never got promoted higher than a GS-13 pay scale. My 29 years of government experience was comparable to sitting in the back seat of a segregated bus." I want to help anyone experiencing discrimination in any environment. Take a ride with me as I tell my story and learn how I was able to thrive against job discrimination, become an entrepreneur, receive a doctorate degree, and become a best-selling author.

My Early Years

My journey began as any other ordinary Black child growing up on the south-side of Chicago. I grew up in a middle-class two-parent household. My mother and father instilled me with a strong work ethic. Thankfully, they also believed in me and provided me with self-confidence and self-worth. They also taught me to have faith in my skills and abilities and to have faith in Allah.

These values are what helped me to overcome the discrimination I faced on the job. My parents taught me that I would "almost" always reap the benefits of my labor if I stayed in school and worked hard. They also told me that life would not always be fair, and that racial discrimination still played a large role in the lives of many Black Americans. Despite knowing these adversities, I pursued my goal of working in the field of business.

I attended college and majored in Business Management with a minor in Marketing. Marketing was always my first love. I eventually landed a job with the Federal Government as a Contracting Officer (CO). While working as a CO, I obtained my MBA. I was able to somewhat advance my career and land my dream job as a Marketing Project Manager, with no supervisory duties.

However, my career came to a sudden halt as I began to apply for managerial positions. I was about to get my first dose of job discrimination.

In the context of civil rights law, "unlawful discrimination refers to unfair or unequal treatment of an individual (or group) based on certain characteristics," (Find.law.com).

These characteristics include age disability, ethnicity, gender marital status, national origin, race, religion, and sexual orientation.

Unfair and Unequal Treatment

I began working at the federal government in the early 1990s. I enjoyed my job and met some wonderful people both Black and White. The "unfair and unequal" treatment began whenever I applied for a management position. As a Black, Muslim female, managerial promotions were totally out of the question in an environment still dominated by White male management.

According to a 2018 study published by LeanIn.Org and McKinsey & Co., Black women receive 39% less pay than white men and 21% less than white women (Black Enterprise, 2019). The article also states that pay disparity exists even if black women do the same work and have the same level of education as White men and women.

Many of my White male and female counterparts who were hired around the same year that I was hired were eventually promoted to Branch Chiefs and Directors within 10 years. They had the advantage of a good ol' boy network to help mentor them; even if they had no idea what they were doing. I remember training some new white employees who soon passed me by.

As an experienced Marketing Manager with an MBA, I applied for several managerial marketing positions at my government job. I often advanced to the interviewing stage, which is not always easy. Each time I applied; I later received an e-mail stating that I was not selected for the job. Every time I inquired about my non-selection; I was told that "I did not score well on my interview." After receiving several non-selections, I finally decided to take action.

I never expected to file an Equal Employment Opportunity Commission (EEOC) case when I first began my government career. I also never expected to be treated so unfairly. As a well-known Reverend once stated in the eulogy of a 46-year-old unarmed Black man killed by white police officers on May 25, 2020, in Minneapolis Minnesota: *"Just take the knee off my neck."*

My comparison is not as deadly or horrific as the Minnesota incident, yet the motives behind discrimination are the same. To halt or kill the lives of Black Americans. In my case, I was prohibited from moving up the government ladder because of my race, gender, and religion.

Non-Selection

My first non-selection was for a team leader position that was never announced. No one in our department was given the opportunity to apply for the job. The White wife of a White Director got the job. She was afforded the white privilege so many White men and women receive yet kept secret. She worked right beside me, and we were both doing the same work, yet she had received a secret promotion and was getting paid more than all the other Project Managers in the same department. I later found out that she had been secretly promoted for an entire year after filing my first EEOC complaint. There were many cases that followed.

My last non-selection case involved a White male panelist scoring only half of my responses from my "structured interview." The interview consisted of 10 pre-determined job-related questions. The Lead White panel member only scored five out of my 10 questions. When my attorney inquired about the discrepancies, we were told that he "had planned to fill in the scores later." Who does that?

It was obvious that this White manager had no intention of giving me the job. My responses were not important enough to even score. The other two "so-called" Black panel members had blackened out my original scores. The blackouts revealed that the higher scores were later changed to mimic the lower scores of the White Lead panel member. My interviews were fixed from the start.

Loopholes and Retaliation

I learned that structured interviews should follow government-issued best practices. Best practices state that panel members should meet before interviews are conducted and decide, which responses receive scores 1-5, with 5 being the highest. In other words, the "correct" responses should be determined before the interviewing stage and not during the interviews.

Pre-determined scoring ensures that interviews are conducted on an equal basis for all applicants. White management never followed these recommended procedures. This was the "loophole." According to Webster's Dictionary (2020), a loophole is 1) a means of escape 2) an ambiguity or omission in the text through which the intent of a statute, contract, or obligation may be evaded. The interviewing process is one of the loopholes that ensured discriminatory hiring. This method allowed white mangers to continue to hire and promote preferred White male and female applicants. There are always loopholes in systemic racism. Similar to how racist cops justify killing unarmed, Black men and women by saying that they "feared for their lives."

Painful Memories

It was during my EEOC filings and depositions that I felt alone and isolated at my job.

I felt as if there was a sign that was posted on my forehead that said, "stay away she's trouble." My other Black and Latino co-workers were also unhappy with how promotions were being conducted but were too afraid to speak up. Fear is cripplingly and silence equals complicity.

However, I could not blame my co-workers for not speaking up. As government employees, we have exciting careers, wonderful benefits, and families to support. I loved my job and having to file a complaint was not easy for me. Yet, being quiet while suffering a lack of job promotions was slowly killing me, and I chose to live. It became a matter of principle, and unlike my co-workers, I could not remain silent.

I asked one Black female co-worker who had received the exact same injustices as myself to join me in my fight. She was too afraid and told me that she would pray over the situation and that she only wanted peace. A few years later she was fired for low performance. The last time we spoke she was homeless and needed psychiatric assistance. Losing a good paying job when you are so close to retirement can be devastating.

I endured many months of filing complaints and paid thousands of dollars to attorneys.

I spent many nights researching cases, answering depositions, and meeting with angry and vindictive tax paid government attorneys. One hateful and spiteful government attorney issued a FOIA to secure documents of my family-owned business. My social media accounts were scrutinized. I also had to fight to get decent performance appraisals. I can strongly identify with the NFL player who protested on bended knee.

I hid my pain at work. Only a few co-workers knew what was going on in my life. I was ostracized and emotionally beat down for speaking up against discrimination. How dare I fight against white privilege? I lost a few cases and I settled a few cases. Settling was winning in my book and I never lost hope.

Family and Faith

During these painful years, my main source of hope came from the comfort of my family. My mother, sister, and son were my inspiration and guiding light. My family's love and support helped me to stay strong during my ordeal. My family and my faith got me through my troubled waters. My early years of having self-confidence, self-worth, and faith gave me the strength to endure and thrive. I also joined a support group consisting of other government employees nationwide who had endured similar discrimination in their Federal jobs. I learned that I was not alone, and I felt empowered. Although I fought with despair, I also persevered in new directions. It was during these turbulent times that my life took a turn in a new direction: A direction that changed my life of pain to a life of freedom.

Transformational Journey

My transformation journey began when I started my family business of assisting adults with developmental and intellectual disabilities. My suffering from job discrimination was coming to an end as I began thriving as an entrepreneur. I decided to steer my passion for equality and justice into helping those who could not fight for themselves.

I also wanted to further my education and decided to pursue an advanced degree in business. While still fighting the good fight, I achieved a Doctorate Degree in Organizational Leadership. This is when I learned about critical thinking and most importantly, I learned about Emotional Intelligence (EI). This was my epiphany moment, my turning point. I truly believe that Allah wanted me to help others learn how to stand up against adversity and racism through the principles of EI.

EI Stress and the RISKE Method

Emotional intelligence (EI) is "the ability to (a) perceive emotion, (b) use emotion to facilitate thought, (c) understand emotions and (d) manage emotion," (Mayer & Salovey, 1993, p. 48). My dissertation was titled: "The relationship between stress and emotional intelligence among direct-care workers," (Karriem, 2010). The results revealed that the higher a person's level of EI, the lower their level of stress and vice versa. In other words, if you can control your emotions, then you can control your stress. Increasing my EI levels, gave me the ability to think clearly, and focus on empowerment. Discrimination on the job was no longer stressing me out. I learned that challenges can sometimes be a blessing in disguise.

My story is my testimony of how obstacles can transform into blessings. We all have the power to transform our lives. Each day we wake up is the chance for a new beginning. I have labeled this transformational process as the RISKE method. I created this method to survive against obstacles. This method can be used by anyone to help improve your quality of life.

We must take risks in order to reach our goals. The RISKE method is based on these five principles.

1. **(R)** Recognize the Problem. What are the issues(s)?

2. **(I)** Instill Prayer and Meditation. What Spiritual methods do you use to cope?

3. **(S)** Seek Solutions. List solutions to your issues.

4. **(K)** Know your Worth. What are your strengths and weaknesses?

5. **(E)** Evoke Emotional Intelligence. How are you managing your emotions?

I created a workbook, which outlines how these principles work to enable you to overcome obstacles in life. I am still a work in progress and often refer to these principles as needed. This workbook can help ease the suffering of discrimination or any other adversities.

In conclusion, I was able to thrive against job discrimination and become an entrepreneur, receive a doctorate degree, and become a best-selling author. The RISKE method has enabled me to escape the plantation and become a free Black Muslim woman. Adversity and racism are a part of life, but so is happiness and success. The faster we can manage our emotions and process them, the faster we can empower ourselves and move into a new zone of joy and bliss.

References:

Black Enterprise (2019): *The Women in the Workplace.* Retrieved August 18, 2020, from https://www.blackenterprise.com/black-women-less-likely-to-be-promoted-receive-recognition-for-accomplishments/amp/

Find Law.com. *What is Discrimination?* Retrieved August 18, 2020, from:

https://civilrights.findlaw.com/civil-rights-overview/what-is-discrimination.html

Karriem, Keesha L (2010). *The relationship between stress and emotional intelligence among direct-care workers.* University of Phoenix, ProQuest Dissertations Publishing, 2010. 3411125. Retrieved August 22, 2020, from https://pqdtopen.proquest.com/doc/520517190.html?FMT=ABS

Mayer, J., Salovey, P., & Caruso, D. (2004). Emotional intelligence: Theory, findings, and implications. *Psychological Inquiry, 15*(3), 197-215. Retrieved August 20, 2020, from EBSCO host database.

Webster's Dictionary (2020). Retrieved August 20, 2020, from https://www.merriam-webster.com/dictionary/loophole

AGAINST ALL ODDS

Tiffani Teachey

Despite all of the obstacles, we may go through in our lives, we have to go through a test in order to have a testimony. Women are underrepresented in Science, Technology, Engineering, and Math (STEM) fields and many have experienced gender discrimination. As an African-American female with an engineering background, representation matters and I can attest to the importance of increasing diversity and closing the gender gap in a male-dominated field of STEM. I want to encourage and inspire more women to consider themselves or even encourage more of our young ladies to consider going into STEM fields. Come with me on this journey as I discuss going from a curious young girl to a powerful role model in STEM.

You are Enough

It starts as early as elementary school when many young girls start to think that they are not smart enough, especially in math and science classes, and boys continue to think that they are skilled. It is these same girls that can grow up to become women that are discouraged from pursuing so-called stereotypical male-dominated careers specifically in STEM. There is a lack of interest at times with many girls and women in science and engineering fields. There remains a common belief, that men are mathematically superior and a better fit for STEM fields than women. Therefore, it leaves a lack of representation and diversity, which leads to a lack of talent when it comes to women and underrepresented minorities wanting to pursue STEM fields.

According to the National Girls Collaborative Project, men vastly outnumber women majoring in most STEM fields in college, and women make up only 28% of the workforce in STEM (NSF, Science & Engineering Indicators, 2018). During life, some women deal with "imposter syndrome," which means having a disbelief in one's own accomplishments and abilities. Intellectual self-doubt begins to sink in with women as they start to doubt if they could be good enough when it comes to their careers, especially in STEM. There are benefits to women being a part of STEM fields. One example is that they can bring a unique perspective to STEM conversations. They are able to utilize their analytical and problem-solving skills and influence societal change with an inclusive world.

If You Believe It, Then You Can Achieve It

I grew up with an entrepreneurial dad and teacher mom. I am the oldest child and I have a younger brother. My brother and I were able to be exposed to so much growing up. I was able to take part in sports (basketball, volleyball, track), music (guitar, piano, alto saxophone), and made sure to excel in academics, (National Honors Society). I was well-rounded and made sure to take part in any opportunity that was given to me, no matter the obstacles that may have come my way. My parents instilled in us the value of service and giving back, the importance of working hard, having a solid education, and if I believe it, then I can achieve it.

There were times in my math and science classes, where I would be the young girl that sat at the front of the class, constantly asking questions, especially when I knew others in the class didn't understand. I learned that many of the boys in the class pretended like they knew the math or science lessons, however, they had the same questions and challenges at times. There is value in having parents that are involved in a child's life when it comes to their education. There was a moment in school, where a math teacher may have had a bad day and took it out on me by yelling at me when I asked a math question that day.

I felt defeated and discouraged, especially with it being in my math class and I shared this discontent with my mom. Well, my mom being a teacher herself, didn't like what she heard and came to the school and expressed her concern with the math teacher. My mom told the math teacher that I can ask questions in class and shouldn't be apprehended for asking questions. As it turns out, the math teacher was having a bad day and apologized. Ultimately, I excelled in math and am grateful to have parents that encouraged me to stand up for my education. Initially, I wanted to be a lawyer because I thought I could debate. However, I did not realize early on my math and science capabilities. It was my parents that made sure my brother and I participated in various math and science scholastic programs. We would go to a Math and Science Saturday Academy, which gave us the tools necessary to utilize our problem-solving skills. It also was the beginning of considering engineering as a career and major.

With my mom being a teacher and understanding the value of an education, she was able to make sure we were connected to the right educational programs necessary to succeed. It was through social capital, that my dad had a client, a civil engineer that shared with him the importance of my brother and me considering engineering as a major. Both my brother and I decided to become engineers with the help of my parents who reminded us that we can be anything we put our minds to.

When I decided to move forward into engineering, I actually went in undecided. It gave me the opportunity to determine which of the various types of engineering that I wanted to major in. I decided on mechanical engineering. During my college journey, I was surrounded by predominantly male classmates. There was a low number of women in the field of engineering. One day in class, the professor said, look to the left and then look to the right, not many of us will make it through the class. I still overcame the challenges of naysayers.

I was well-rounded on campus, served as a resident advisor, and took part in various internships. It was through participating in engineering organizations such as the Society of Women Engineers (SWE) and the National Society of Black Engineers (NSBE), that aided in shaping my future in graduating with my Bachelor of Science in Engineering as well as a Master of Science in Engineering Management. The journey was not easy, however, it challenged me as an African-American female engineer in a male-dominated field. As a young engineer out of school, I struggled with imposter syndrome and felt as if I had to prove myself and my competence at times. There was a moment when I walked into a small conference room with a vendor for a project. He shook hands with every male in the room. It was then that I realized I was the only female in the room, and he didn't acknowledge me nor shake my hand. I felt as though he may have thought I was an administrative assistant. So, I reached across the table, shook his hand, and shared with him that I was the engineer responsible for the project and that I would be a part of the process in deciding if we would utilize his equipment for the project. The initial action from the vendor disappointed me and I did not appreciate his level of disrespect.

However, after my response to him, I felt empowered by being able to let him know not only my contribution, and I provided awareness to his mishap in not acknowledging my presence in the room. Despite the various challenges and awareness that comes with being in a male-dominated field, it shows me the importance of and need for more women in STEM fields to have a seat at the table.

Becoming the STEM Changer

I went from being a curious young girl to a powerful role model in STEM. I am considered today as the STEM Changer because of my passion for encouraging and being an example for girls and women to consider STEM fields. After 16 years in engineering, I am passionate about encouraging more girls and women to go into STEM as shown through becoming a bestselling author in *What Can I Be? STEM Careers from A to Z* children's book as well as serving as a youth mentor.

Many of my STEM contributions have been recognized through my college alma mater in which I received the Black Alumni Chapter Excellence in Leadership with STEM award and my company recognized me on International Women's Day to celebrate Women's Achievements. With it being Engineers Week and Introducing a Girl to Engineering Day, it was exciting to be featured by the FabFem, a directory that includes an international database of women in science, technology, engineering, and mathematics (STEM) professions who are inspiring role models for young women. The FabFem Directory is accessible to young women, girl-serving STEM programs, and other organizations that are working to increase career awareness and interest in STEM.

Being a STEM change agent and activating my network has helped me to get my voice heard and getting a seat at the table for STEM opportunities. I learned to take advantage of the following tools: access, opportunity, exposure, and knowledge; which led to the success of my STEM journey and to become the STEM Changer.

4 Steps to Get Girls and Women into STEM

1. **Gain access to STEM resources/representatives** – Seek literature about science, technology, engineering, and mathematics with high-quality text and pictures as well as non-traditional STEM materials that can be used in STEM explorations. Highlighting women that have and continue to make contributions to this world helps in representation in STEM for girls and women.

2. **Take advantage of opportunities to connect with Mentors/ Sponsors** – Learning the difference between a mentor and sponsor and getting both can be essential to nurturing interest in STEM fields, as well as help build girls and women's confidence. Mentors can provide advice and can help expand girls and women's networks. Sponsors can

advocate and speak on one's behalf when they are not in the room. It is also important to understand the value of one's circle of influence. Girls and women should surround themselves with positive people that are striving to be the best in life.

3. **Expose girls earlier to STEM** – This will aid in combating gender bias in girls and women. Focusing more on how engineering and coding can be innovative problem-solving can combat the stigma and barriers of having to be good at math and science when it comes to pursuing STEM fields. Participating in hands-on work at home or school activities through various STEM experiments, can influence the decision for girls and women to pursue STEM fields.

4. **Become knowledgeable of various STEM Programs** – Research is key. There are various STEM organizations such as the Society of Women Engineers and minority groups such as the National Society of Black Engineers that offer STEM programs and activities. There are after school programs, STEM camps, and school activities tied to STEM that can be encouraging and open the eyes and minds for girls to be exposed to STEM. Girls and women can learn more about the different possibilities in the STEM fields by participating in various companies and organizations summer internships, job shadowing programs, and/or career days.

Representation Matters

I want my legacy to be that I was able to make a difference in this world and one of them is that I was known for sharing the importance of representation matters in STEM. It is my hope that through sharing my STEM journey that more women and girls are encouraged to go into STEM fields because there is a need for more diversity and a seat at the table in STEM. The world will succeed when new discoveries and possibilities are unlocked with more diversity and inclusion in STEM fields. Against all odds we are overcomers and it is through access, opportunity, exposure, and knowledge that girls and women can become powerful and impactful women in STEM.

SELF-WORTH EMPOWERMENT

"I must undertake to love myself and to respect myself as though my very life depends upon self-love and self-respect."

-Maya Angelou

POWERLESS TO POWERFUL

TrevisMichelle

Thistory was not supposed to be my reality. As a young teenager, I had it all planned out. I would love my children, my husband, maintain a loving environment, and never get divorced. My household would be healthy, happy, and made of dreams. Being young, and full of hope made me think this dream would become my reality. If you are reading this, then you know that the dream and reality crashed and burned. Come along with me on this journey as I take you from the powerlessness of divorce, to how I took my power back!

The Root of Powerlessness

According to *Psychology Today*, women feel powerless at times because they don't know how to feel comfortable exercising their power and may believe that they are perceived as mean and angry when voicing their opinions. A lot of women are dependent on others for their survival. Approximately 1.4 billion women are unemployed. When this occurs, they are subject to the wills and control of men, but when divorce or death happens to the man, they are at high-risk to remain in poverty. I can relate because I was one of them.

Divorce is always a shocker, even though I was present during the process, getting to that point was still surreal. I ask myself how did I get here? What happened? How could I have avoided this? What could I have done differently? How did I allow my power to be taken away?

Beginning of Powerlessness

The journey to divorce has had many twists and turns for me. When my parents' separation led to divorce while attending private school, I was bullied and became the butt of jokes. I learned at an early age to disappear into the background and not make any noise. And how to get through the day, especially while not having any friends. You see I was treated as a pariah and no one wanted to be associated with me, nor did the teachers support or protect me.

My mother took her frustrations, anger, and pain out on me verbally, physically, mentally, and emotionally. She told me one evening that I would never come between her and her man. I was nine-years-old, and my father paid child support and private school tuition while making a conscious decision to see me occasionally. His excuse was that my mother was so mean he did not want to be bothered. Again, I was shown that I was not valued, nor important to either of them. Powerless.

The time I lived with my mother made me feel unloved, a nuisance, and definitely unimportant. My mother and father were alike, although they would not admit it to themselves or anyone else. When I would come back home from visiting my father, when he would show up, my parents would curse and argue in front of me. I tried to go to my room and hide, but it did not work because my mother would find me and take her anger/frustration out on me by beating me, calling me names, not allowing me to hug her, and pretty much ignore me until she needed a task performed.

On the other hand, when I lived with my grandparents, I was loved, made to feel important, and quite frankly, doted on. I spent time talking to my grandparents about my dreams and expectations while receiving a lot of hugs and kisses. I went to church with my grandparents every Sunday, attending Sunday school, and then going to eat at my favorite place, IHOP.

My grandparents knew my mother had a temper and maybe was not loving toward me, but my grandmother would say, "She is hurting. She will grow out of it and she will change. Continue to love her anyway." Life in my grandparent's house was safe and loving. I witnessed a caring and loving couple, learning through their example of what a loving marriage should look and feel like. My dream marriage.

Becoming a teenage mother at the age of 17 after being raped for two years by my mother's live-in boyfriend in Florida, further induced the feelings of powerlessness and being devalued. I subsequently dropped out of Bethune Cookman College, a historically black college university (HBCU) in Daytona Beach, Florida, and moved back to New York to live with my grandparents.

Let me tell you about my journey from low self-esteem, self-doubt, and insecurity as a child to a woman, who is able to take back the power that was stripped from me. I am going to give strategies to women to help them survive their divorce while maintaining their sanity.

Being raped by my mother's boyfriend, and her abuse towards me, left me feeling powerless. This set the stage for me to be in a marriage where I had absolutely no power. It felt normal. I made the decision to remain powerless and not use my voice due to fears and insecurities.

Marrying Powerlessness

Marrying a man in my early 20's who was 52-years-old with children older than me, was going to be my opportunity to have my dream marriage. I knew this marriage would be my first and last because there was no way I was going to put me and my children through a divorce.

Marriage did not end up being all that I thought it would be. In addition to being in charge of my children and my household chores, learning how to be a wife to a much older man was not easy. He expected me to know my role as a wife, mother, and lover. I did not feel comfortable in the latter role. I had to sometimes read books and fake that I knew more than I did.

I began feeling as if I did not have a voice when my opinions were invalidated or ignored. Trying to reason with him and be a partner in the marriage would cause him displeasure. He would chastise me, make fun of me and my thoughts, and then when I would become offended, he would say, "I'm joking, don't be so sensitive." I remember my father doing the same thing, which made me feel unimportant, less than, and quite frankly, stupid at times.

During the beginning years of the marriage, I did not realize he was molding me into the woman he wanted and one he could control. I would hear his friends make these same comments when they thought I was out of earshot. I would find myself agreeing with him so I could keep the peace in the household. Over time, this made my voice eventually become so small it disappeared. This brought back the feelings of powerlessness I felt as a teenager living with my mother and her boyfriend.

One day I made the conscious decision to tell him how I felt and report that I was leaving with the children. This shook him. He listened and promised to make changes...all of the usual actions one says when they don't want you to leave. This lasted for about six months and then the behavior returned. The intimidation and belittling became worse, and on one occasion, he shoved me into a wall while pregnant.

At that moment, I decided I was going to leave no matter what, but I had no money of my own. You see, I quit my job to be a stay-at-home mom when I found out I was pregnant. Of course, this was my husband's idea. He tried to sweeten me up by giving in to my requests (Volvo wagon, travel with my girlfriend to Brazil, and an allowance for the year). I did not believe he would agree, but he did, and I realized later that this was part of his plan...complete control.

Since I was not financially independent, I could not afford to leave. In the interim, I decided to go to school to become a Registered Nurse. I needed a way to support my children since I knew I could not stay. He was all for it until his friends started getting in his head and telling him that I was using him and would leave as soon as I graduated. He would interrupt my studies, on a daily basis. I moved downstairs to the living room and started sleeping on the couch, thinking that this would keep him at bay. That did not work.

Some days I was up all night arguing with him while trying to study. It seemed as though he wanted me to fail so that I would have to stay and not end the marriage.

Feelings of anger, hurt, and failure filled my spirit. I was angry because I was questioning why I could not hold this marriage together. It was my dream to stay married. I was hurt because I tried loving a man with all my heart and I was not enough. I felt like a failure because I could not even be successful in marriage, which in turn made me feel like I failed as a mother. This is definitely not the way I envisioned my marriage turning out.

Making the decision to leave was my first step toward regaining my power and reigniting my voice. I had to strategize how I was going to leave, where I would live, and how I would support myself and my children.

Once I snapped out of the victim mindset, my survivor skills kicked in. The fact that I survived rape, an abusive mother, neglectful father, and being bullied in school, I knew no matter how hard this might be, I could get through it.

At that point, I sat down with pen and paper and wrote out the strategies needed to start the divorce journey. On my list were housing, monthly budget, transportation, tuition, and lawyers' fees.

While going through the process, I sometimes felt as though I wouldn't make it, it was too hard, but I could not give up. At times, I had to bite my tongue, take the high road, and give in to things that were not worth fighting for (furniture, alternating weekend changes, part of his pension, name-calling, and a woman and her daughter threatening me).

When I was at my lowest, in spite of what I was going through, I kept my children in Sunday school, along with making sure that they saw their father as often as possible, to the point of disobeying the court order stating that he should not see them. I put us all in therapy. I continued to love them fiercely, even when they would push me away. I knew one day they would forgive me and their hurt feelings would heal.

Standing up for myself, while consciously staying present, allowed me to find my power. I didn't need approval from my mother or father, since I had my own approval and the love and support of my grandparents. It seemed as though a light bulb came on and began to shine when I started nursing school. Being around other powerful, intelligent women who were supportive, empowered me to achieve on an intellectual and emotional level.

The Power Process

I was powerless in my marriage because I was familiar with having my power stripped in my youth. However, I was able to take back my power, without asking for permission. When you are going through a divorce, it is important to take the following steps:

1. Acknowledge that this is the best decision for you and your children (if you are a parent);

2. Seek God and/or meditate on your decision;

3. Forgive yourself for the part you played in the marriage (good or bad);

4. Seek professional help (therapy, counseling for you and/ or the children);

5. Do not call the father out of his name and/or put him down in front of or to the children (they will think you feel the same about them);

6. Recognize that friends and people will choose sides (including your family);

7. Be mindful of your circle of friends (everyone is not your friend);

8. Give yourself time to grieve (recognize this is a loss);

9. Make time for you (relaxation, affirmations, and rejuvenation);

10. Forgive your husband (this allows you to take back your power).

Repeat these steps daily, which will lead you to a more powerful state of mind.

It is important for you to know that you can and will make it through this journey one day at a time. If I can do it, so can you. I have learned to, "Dream bigger than your thoughts and let your thoughts be bigger than your dreams." (TrevisMichelle)

Today me and my ex-husband are friends. He has since apologized for the part he played in the marriage, telling me that I was a good wife and mother to our children. In fact, I am one of his healthcare proxies. Who would have thought this day would ever come? We may not be married, but we were able to heal, forgive, and move forward as friends. We also have three children who have grown up to become productive and emotionally healthy adults.

Know and believe in your heart that you will also be triumphant. When you make the decision to take back your power, you have put yourself on a trajectory for success...nothing can stop you now.

SEXY AFTER DIVORCE

Lisa Lamazzi

Are you ready to get your sexy back?

Many women experience low self-esteem and low confidence after divorce. I know because I experienced this. Come on this journey with me. I was someone who was not confident, insecure, and didn't know what I wanted in life and in a partner. I went from being in an unhappy marriage to being a powerful, sexy, confident, inspirational speaker and coach and 100% ready to meet the man of my dreams!

Sexy means ... a special *kind* of attraction.

Usually, though, the word 'sexy' is used to mean an additional quality of attraction, a *different* kind of attraction. So you could describe a woman as 'beautiful' without meaning 'sexy.' This is not about the *degree* of attractiveness but about the *kind* of attractiveness. A woman might be exceptionally beautiful but present herself in a way that people would not describe as 'sexy.' Another woman might be plain-looking but present herself in a way that people would describe as 'sexy.' When used about a woman, 'sexy' usually means something about her manner of presentation that is the kind of thing that would have *a distinctive appeal to men*. Sexy equals a woman's confidence and how comfortable she is in her own skin. (Man + Women Magazine)

All too often, people who get **divorced** have feelings of guilt and shame. The trauma of **divorce** can drastically alter your perceptions, feelings, and expectations about relationships and your future. It's easy to lose the essence of yourself without getting support from family friends or mental health professionals. (Mar 17, 2017, Google)

An article from *Psychology Today* dated August 17, 2016, states that divorce is painful, and it has a negative impact on self-esteem. Women think of a divorce as a failure.

- » They grieve what they lost

- » They let their emotions drive their behavior

- » They feel guilty for their kid

- » The uncertainty and insecurity that divorce creates can leave you with an open wound subject to infection. This infection — low self-esteem — can then manifest itself in self-abusive behavior such as:

- » drinking to excess

- » promiscuity (or dating inappropriate people)

- » pill-popping (over-the-counter or prescription meds)

- » starving yourself to be thin — or overeating to comfort yourself

- » staying in a toxic work situation

Make sure you get professional help if you feel an "infection" coming on. – (Article from Divorcemagazine.com)

I was born and raised in Chicago, Illinois. I am the middle child, I have an older brother, Joe, and a younger sister, Lindsay. My parents got a divorce when I was 8-years-old. My father requested that my brother live with him and my sister and I live with my Mom. My mom agreed and we saw my Dad on the weekends. As a little girl, I didn't understand what was going on, however, later I discovered I had some resentment towards my Mom and Dad about my brother living with my Dad and not us. Since then, I have resolved this with both of my parents, and we have a great relationship now.

When I was 23-years-old, I moved to Southern California. At 33-years-old, I met a man who would become my husband. We were in lust and fell in love immediately. I did not know what I wanted in a relationship and I did not know what my non-negotiables were. All I knew is that I wanted to get married and have babies so nothing else mattered; about three years after meeting, we got married in Seal Beach, CA.

Marital Bliss

Before I got married, I ignored the warning signs in my relationship. I knew he was an alcoholic, but I thought I could change him after we got married and he would want to slow down and start a family. However, I was wrong and my happily ever after didn't seem so happy. I was unhappy in my marriage, I felt alone and sad. The main problem I feel we had was his drinking. Alcoholism ran in my husband's family, but he was in denial that he had a problem and did not believe in the AA system. I thought, like many other women, that when we get married, I can change him. He will want to stop drinking and focus on having a family, but I was wrong.

Determined To Win

Nothing was working in my marriage. One big problem was his drinking. I gave him many chances to stop drinking. He tried and wasn't able to stick with it. He tried not drinking at all, that didn't work. I tried to get him to commit to drinking beer; it would never last. I tried to get us both to stop drinking and that never worked. We tried counseling and that didn't work. We started to grow apart from each other. I then realize I need to focus on saving myself and make my own life work. Another problem I had in my marriage was that I felt alone and I always craved partnership.

I worked hard on several businesses on the side to build an additional income for our family and he didn't have an interest in ever helping me. He was always upset. I was on the phone doing business at all hours of the day and not giving him enough quality time. His love language was quality time and mine was words of affirmation. I never gave him quality time and he never acknowledged me for anything good I was doing. I was determined to make my marriage work. I indulged myself in personal growth workshops hoping to improve our communication and work through our problems. We went to counseling and that didn't work. He was resistant to doing these workshops with me but to make me happy he did some. However, it didn't work.

Scary Times

One morning, I received a phone call from my father-in-law, and he said my mother-in-law fell and was bleeding profusely and was being rushed to the hospital and he didn't know if she was going to make it. I immediately called my husband and told him I was coming to pick him up from work so we can go straight to the hospital. Now, I'm going to be completely honest here, I don't feel good about saying this, but this was the straw that broke the camel's back. This is when I knew I was unhappy and that I had to do something about it. The one and only thought that was going through my head while driving to the hospital was that if my mother-in-law died, how was I going to be able to leave my husband? I mean what person would do that if someone lost their Mom and then lost their wife? I started wondering how I was going to be in an unhappy marriage for the rest of my life and I was scared.

For Better or For Worse?

It turned out that she was fine and was able to come home and we took care of her in her recovery. Shortly after that event, I mustered up the courage to have a conversation with my husband again that I was leaving, and this time was for good. I was 39-years-old at the time. Before my 40th birthday, I left my husband and told him I want a divorce. I left everything to him except my aero bed and my alkaline water machine. I moved in with one of my best friend's Jill and slept in her room on my aero bed on her floor. It was the hardest decision that I ever made.

How Will I Survive?

A few weeks after I did that, I got laid off from my job. Everything started to crumble...I hit rock bottom, and I lost it all. I didn't have the confidence to look for another job. I felt guilty and ashamed that I was breaking my word to forever, through thick and thin.

There was a lot of judgment going on even with my friends that I thought were on my side. I was embarrassed by what other people thought because we looked like a perfect couple on the outside and on Facebook. No one knew what went on behind closed doors after he was drinking, a lot of verbal and mental abuse.

The shame I felt was a hard pill to swallow. It was hard to get up out of bed, I was depressed and was not motivated to do anything. However, I made myself workout because that was the only thing that made me feel good mentally and physically.

I was someone who was not confident, insecure, and didn't know what I wanted in life and in a partner. I went from being in an unhappy marriage to being a powerful, sexy, confident, inspirational speaker and coach and 100% ready to meet the man of my dreams!

Here are the steps I took:

1. **Forgiveness.** Forgive yourself, forgive your ex, and let go of resentment and anger so you can take responsibility for your part of why your marriage did not work. This is making a phone call, writing a letter, and creating a friendship!

2. **Grieve.** Allow yourself to grieve what you lost. Embrace your sadness, it's ok. If you refuse to acknowledge the good times (and surely there were good times), then those feelings of grief will follow you until you do.

3. **Personal Growth.** Register yourself in a workshop that assists you in removing barriers/limiting beliefs from your past that are in the way of making your dreams come true in every area of life. Create a dream board and put it on your wall in your bedroom to look at every day of what you want your life to look like.

4. **Self-Care.** Take care of yourself. Prioritize your health. Get massages, pamper yourself with manicures and/or pedicures. Schedule an appointment with your doctor to bring your health to an optimal level. Spend lots of time with your closest girlfriends that care about you.

5. **Detox the Mind.** Get rid of unhealthy and toxic thoughts and gain your energy back. Meditate daily, prayer, write in a journal daily your thoughts and feelings that come up on your journey. Listen to positive affirmations.

6. **Detox your Body.** You can take a daily bubble bath with lavender Epsom salt at night. Do a juice cleanse to get rid of all the toxins in your body and have a fresh start. Find some natural healthy, organic supplements to slowly but surely wing yourself off any medications that you are taking. (Talk to your dietician/doctor for recommendations).

7. **Challenge Yourself.** Register yourself in a marathon, triathlon, spartan race, mud run, or a bikini/fitness competition like I did, or, if that's not your thing, pick something that will challenge you outside your comfort zone. Pick something that you've always wanted to do and you were too scared to do it and immerse yourself in it.

I hope my story was inspirational and it's calling you in action to fulfill your dreams. If you are going through a divorce or already divorced, then I hope this motivates you to build up your self-esteem, confidence, and help you get your sexy back!

Visit my website at www.sexyafterdivorce.com or on Facebook and Instagram at Sexy After Divorce.

Drop me a message and let me know how things are going for you.

IDENTITY

Jacinta Wolff BSN, RN

Who are you... do you know? Many people appear to have everything together on the outside, deep down they have been struggling like you and me. Identity is extremely important to know and develop or we will feel lost in the world and not be able to adapt to changes in our lives. I lost my identity at an early age and it took me a great amount of time to find the woman that was hidden all these years. I would like to help other women to find their identity, so they find their passion in life. Come with me on my personal journey of how I came from being lost in my identity to finding myself, so I could be truly happy with the woman I am today.

We as individuals need to be strong in our identities to be able to handle what life throws at us. Many of us have children that rely on us to be strong no matter what happens. Children learn by example, so we all need to take the time to find ourselves as individuals to help the younger generation learn to be confident in their identity. There was a research study from LinkedIn and it was polled in the United States, United Kingdom, India, and Australia found that 75% of 25- 33-year-olds have experienced a quarter-life crisis. (New LinkedIn Research Shows 75 Percent of 25-33-Year-olds Have Experienced Quarter-life Crises, 2017).

The psychologist Erik Erikson came up with the term "identity crisis." (Krauss Whitbourne, 2012) Erikson believed that our personalities are developed by going through and resolving crises in our life. (Elmer, 2018) So, when you think of an identity crisis we often think of this as a negative connotation when in reality, if faced correctly, it can give us a stronger sense of who we are as an individual. Throughout our lives, it is normal to feel this way as we change and grow into adulthood. We all face different adversities in our lives, but it is how we handle them that makes us all unique. (New LinkedIn Research Shows 75 Percent of 25-33-Year-Olds Have Experienced Quarter-life Crises, 2017). Well, enough about numbers let's start this marathon journey I call life and see how I went from being confused and lost to found and confident in my identity.

The Marathon Called Life

I was born and raised in Columbus, Ohio where I was the oldest of seven children. I am a divorced mother of four children, two girls who are 25 and 23, and two boys that are 21 and 20. I am also a cardiac step-down nurse, a flutist who has played in the church since the age of 12 and plays for weddings. I love to exercise, enjoy nature, and spend time with friends and family. I love to inspire people to truly find themselves and find out what makes them happy and get true fulfillment out of life.

Being a child of a large family, we had to have many roles to help the family dynamic. I was the oldest of seven children so, as we got older my parents needed me to help organize and strategize how we would all get everyone to their activities. At an early age, I was given a lot more responsibilities and enjoyed helping make sure things run smoothly in the house. As a result, I lost my identity of being a child and had a hard time finding it. I was not comfortable and confident with who I was as an individual. I always felt I was more mature for my age and enjoyed the company of adults more than children my own age.

I went to a Catholic elementary and high school where I did not fit in. I felt alone and isolated. At a young age, I learned to play the flute and that became my outlet for all my frustrations. I became a part of the folk group who played every week at church. I finally felt accepted somewhere. I relied on my faith and love of God to help me through my sadness and despair and get through my identity crises that have led me to be the woman I am today. At the age of 10, I felt isolated and trapped in my life. I did not fit in at school, I did not feel like I fit in at home. I was not built like my siblings and had a hard time accepting my differences. As I became a teenager, I still had not found my true identity. I was lost, I did not feel like a teenager who was carefree and enjoying life. I struggled to know who I was and just wanted to fit in somewhere. My self-esteem was extremely low, and I didn't love myself. I clung to whoever would accept me. I longed to fit in and be loved.

In the trenches, pounding the pavement

At the age of 17, I got pregnant with a biracial child and was scared of what the future held for me. I knew I would face adversity and was ready to face anything that came my way. My school and my parents made me go to counseling. I was mad and angry that they were forcing this upon me. I was confused about why they all thought I needed help because I was pregnant. At the time I felt like I was letting my parents down by not being a responsible adult even though I was not an adult at all. I always wanted to be a mother but also wanted to be a nurse. I did not do well on my ACT, so I assumed I was not smart enough to go to college. I believe that I wanted to fit in the adult world so badly that I subconsciously was careless and became pregnant on purpose. I continued going to school and graduated with my class.

At the age of 19, I was married, by the time I was 23, I was the mother of four children. I wanted that family dynamic so badly. I believed that being a mother and wife I had found my identity. I loved being a mother and wife. Still, I struggled to know who I was as an individual. I was completely lost but still needed to be strong for my children. For many years, I went through the motions of being a mother and wife but felt trapped, not knowing what to do again! During those years, I would think about my dream of being a nurse and how I gave it up by having my family so young. I felt that was the missing part of my life. I stayed in an emotionally abusive marriage for almost 13 years. I fell further into depression, low self-esteem, and low self-worth that I did not know who I was a person or an individual. I needed to find my identity.

Hitting that runners brick wall

I finally hit that brick wall hard, I was done pretending I was happy with my life, how I was being treated as a wife, and not fulfilling my dream of being a nurse. Being a mother was not my only calling in life, and I was ready to pursue my calling as a nurse. At the age of 33, I got divorced and started working on loving myself and finding out what else I wanted out of life. I loved being a mother, but I needed more. I decided to pursue my dream of becoming a nurse.

While doing that, I found the part of me that was missing. My self-esteem started to increase, and I finally believed in myself. I wanted to show my children to always follow your dreams and never give up on yourself. I fought hard to find my true identity.

Nutritional supplements to get past that wall

Finding the right nutritional supplements to help me find my identity was crucial to get over myself self-doubt, low self-esteem, and depression. When I was at my lowest point, these were the things I did in spite of what I was going through.

1. My faith, prayer, and trust in God helped me to endure the long hours, the studying, and fighting through the pain that my ex-husband put me through while still having to raise my four children. I not only prayed physical prayers, I sang and played my flute at church as another form of prayer, I went to meditation services that concentrated on self-examination and reflection of who I was as a person. I knew I could do anything with God behind me. One of my favorite prayers is the Serenity Prayer, *"God grant me the Serenity to accept the things I cannot change; Courage to change the things I can, and Wisdom to know the difference,"* written by American Theologian Reinhold Niebuhr in 1932.2. Concentrating on the love of my children and wanting better for them and

myself. I wanted to show them that even through adversity you can succeed. 3. By admitting my sadness, fears, and anxiety I was experiencing with my family and friends I was able to face my challenges head-on.

Once my family and friends knew what I was going through, they gave me the encouragement to keep fighting to find the true me and find what it was going to take to find her. My parents were there to support me and help wherever they could. Not everyone has parents that would help with not many questions but, mine did and that was very helpful as well. 4. Exercise and diet were important during this uncertain time. The combination of running, yoga, meditation, and weightlifting helped me in different ways. When I was running, it was my time to think and reflect, which gave me clarity on what was going on and how I was going to handle everything while getting physically stronger.

Yoga and meditation helped me to relax and forget about all my worries, for an hour at a time. I was getting my diet in check and making sure I was eating and getting the nutrition I needed, to do all the work I needed to do to keep a single house going to succeed. 5. I went on a search for my self-affirmation. Self-affirmation is the recognition and assertion of the existence of the value of a person as an individual, which is exactly what I needed to find. For so many years, I had lost who my individual self was, I was the mother, sister, and aunt but who was I as an individual? I sat down and defined characteristics of myself and what I valued in myself. I realized that I was a hard-working, self-motivated woman who values myself as not only a mother but also an individual. Both roles are equally important. Not one role is more important than the other. I would no longer let anyone cause me to doubt who I was and what was important to me. I would stand my ground and make sure that whomever I was involved with would respect me for who I was and what I stood for as a strong single mother.

Perseverance to the Finish Line

I worked full-time while going to school full-time, clinical hours, and still participating in all my children's activities. I wanted them to know I believed in them and supported them in any way possible. I finished with my Bachelor of Science of nursing Magna Cum Laude. I came from being lost in my identity crises to finding myself, as I pushed through the turmoil to find my true identity and became the woman I aspired to be.

Today, I am a strong, beautiful, confident, and smart woman that has found her way! I love myself for who I am and what I stand for in life. I love to help people and I get to do that every day as a nurse. I feel that my patients touch my life as much I touch their lives. I get to touch people's lives and enhance their spiritual experience by sharing my talent of playing flute in the church and at special events I love to stay active and have fulfilled another life dream of finishing a full marathon and five half-marathons.

My children are all strong independent young adults who are finding their way in life. I am such a proud mother and will continue to support my children in all their endeavors in life. It is so important to make sure you take the time to truly find what makes you happy and fulfilled in life.

References

Elmer, J. (2018, October 31). Identity crisis: Definition, symptoms, causes, and treatment.

Healthline. Retrieved July 29, 2020, from https://www.healthline.com/ health/mental-health/identity-crisis

Krauss Whitbourne, S., Ph.D. (2012, March 3). Are you having an identity crisis? www.psychologytoday.com. Retrieved August 18, 2020, from https://www.psychologytoday.com/us/blog/fulfillment-any-age/201203/are-you-having-identity-crisis

New LinkedIn research shows 75 percent of 25-33-year-olds have experienced quarter-life crises. (2017, November 15). https://news.l

Seeking Validation from the Wrong Sources

Charmane West

One comment under a social media post can be all someone needs to start their day. Some young girls validate their beauty based on the number of likes they get. Why is that? It's because they are seeking validation from the wrong places.

Over the past 21 years of nursing, I have encountered people that have become depressed, suicidal, drug-addicted, manipulative, hateful, and abusive as a result of seeking validation from all the wrong sources. Having children, a wonderful marriage, and a career are some of life's greatest gifts. However, it is important to understand who you are first by seeking validation from God so that God's plan for your life will unfold and your true journey will begin.

Self-validation is important for me to talk about because I wasted so much of my precious life trying to be complete or whole if you will. I spent too much of my life seeking approval from people not realizing the importance of knowing who I am first and being comfortable with myself. I came to realize if one does not understand the importance of being able to validate and understand their self-worth, they will waste so much of their life trying to live what they think is their life when in fact they are living someone else's life.

Validation Issues

"In the U.S., almost 70 percent of the adult population uses Facebook, with 90.4 percent of Millennials reporting they are active users. By clicking the thumbs up, posting a comment, or sharing a post, people are validating each other at an increasing rate. This, as well as the need for in-person validation, can create anxiety, depression, and low self-esteem, (Psychology Today.com, Sherry Gaba, LCSW)."

"Validation is part of being interdependent and relying on the feedback and encouragement of others around us. Even independent people still need validation in some aspects of their life; however, they are also able to accept their own self-validation if they do not get it from someone else (Hall, 2012)."

I am discussing seeking validation from the wrong sources because people need to stop depending on validation from others and learn to validate themselves. People need to know the importance of getting to know themselves and loving themselves first before starting serious relationships. Before complicating their lives and the lives of others. I hope my story encourages others to seek validation from within.

My Beginning

I am Charmane Patricia West. My mother was born in the country of Jamaica W.I. married and had two daughters. When I was born this made three.

After twenty years of being in an unhappy marriage, my mother went on to start a new chapter in her life and she left her husband. Mom managed to obtain a visa allowing her to leave the country for business and then return home to Kingston, Jamaica. However, Mom did not return. Mom left Jamaica pregnant with me and she moved to the United States, specifically New York City.

Mom was alone and pregnant. A woman I will call 'E' learned about my mother and she let her live in one of the rooms in her extremely large apartment in Harlem, New York, which also served as her brother's medical practice. She offered my mom a room in the back of the apartment, which was large enough for a queen-size bed, a crib, and a small toilet room with a sink.

This allowed my mother a place to live while she went to work. My mother later went to the famous F.I.T. for fashion and design full-time and worked at night while E ran her brother's practice and raised me. E became like a grandmother and mother to me and I loved her with every ounce of my being.

Sadness

Then that dreadful day came, I was seven-years-old. I had come home from school and my grandmother E sat with the saddest look on her face. She told me it was time for me to leave her and go live in Brooklyn with my mother. I was already a nervous and anxious child. I thought I was about to lose my life and the only person to ever show concern and love towards me. I loved my mother and I instinctively knew they were right, and it was time to leave my beloved adopted grandmother and return with my mother and sisters who were also now in the US. I remember sobbing, sitting on her lap on the toilet crying telling her I would never ever forget her and that I would be back.

My New Normal

I spent the majority of my childhood alone. I was so quiet. My mom and sisters would forget that I was there. My mother spent so much time trying to make up for the many years she lost in my sister's upbringing, she literally had no time for me. My mother was extremely hard working. My mother became a successful designer working for major top designers in the world. She became so successful and moved into a penthouse apartment in Brooklyn Heights, New York. There were no other black families that we ever encountered in the neighborhood at that time. My mother was determined to be successful; she knew what she wanted and the life she wanted to have. However, as a result of her seeking validation from a man that she married and divorced. I don't think she ever got to truly enjoy her life and her daughters.

Seeking Validation

As I grew up, I became anxious around people always in fear of not being liked or misunderstood. My father would call from Jamaica to speak with my sisters, but he would never speak to me. I grew up thinking I was not old enough to speak to my father and that's why he did not speak to me. I spent my entire life waiting to speak to him.

As a child, I would roam the streets of Brooklyn Heights talking to strangers, playing alone, and eventually, when I became a teenager, I felt my life had no meaning or purpose. My first boyfriend was so much in love with me, that I began to feel happiness, and then later I was disappointed by his behavior. I broke up with him and fell in love with my second boyfriend. We both had serious plans to marry and hoped to be together forever and then my first child was born, she was not an accident.

Invalidated

When I was 16-years old, my father died. My mother and my sister packed up and flew to Jamaica to go to the funeral. My mother never explained to me why I was not invited. I later found out by accident that my father who I was raised to believe was my dad, was not my father. This was an emotional time because now I understood why he only sent my sister cards and money. Consequently, I grew up without a father and without the attention of a mother. I was unable to feel a sense of security. I had so many disappointments from people, and I was always seeking validation.

The Beginning of My Transformation

Although I was only 15 when she was born, for the first time in my adolescent life, I wanted to live. My fiancée at the time was immature and I moved on without hesitation because I realized he was incapable of loving me the way I deserved to be loved. The relationship became violent and a constant emotional struggle. I knew I could accomplish anything I put my mind to because I now had a purpose to live. I no longer needed to be in a relationship to realize that my life was important. I stopped trying to please my mother because I felt I was a burden to her.

I always believed in education and I continued to go to school until the Principal and the Assistant Principal from my high school came to my home. They rang the doorbell, I politely let them in. They proceeded to tell me that my grades were not up to par and my future looked grim because I was a teenage mother, and it made no sense to continue high school. I was shocked. I thought I was doing ok. I knew that school was a struggle since I was in kindergarten, I developed social anxiety and school made me uncomfortable. However, I agreed to drop out of high school.

The next day I went up to the school and filled out the necessary papers to withdraw and I enrolled in night school, while I worked days. I lied about my age and I located a nursing agency in the yellow pages, that was located in Lindenhurst, Long Island. I approached the manager at the agency and stated to her that I was looking for work. She said I had to take a test and pass in order to find work. Well I sat down, took the test and I scored 99%. The manager looked at me and said few people come in here and pass this exam on the first try, and she was impressed with my high-test score and recommended that I look into becoming a registered nurse. (I knew God was managing my steps).

I completed high school with an equivalency diploma, and I can tell you I worked hard for it failing the first time and then the second time until I had victory. No one could tell me that their traditional high school diploma was any greater than the high diploma I had received.

I immediately enrolled in Vogue Beauty School in Manhattan and became a licensed cosmetologist by the age of 18. I went to work for a prestigious salon on Park Avenue in New York. And I later studied under John Atchison, where I studied the art of geometric and precision cutting. I studied under some of the most talented designers during that time. I traveled to different states honing my skills and eventually landed a job in London as a platform artist to London's largest Trade show.

I would teach and demonstrate my haircuts; I began to teach salon owners and other stylists in precision cutting and styling. I also got married at the age of 18 and eventually had two more children. By the age of 23, I was the mother of three children and also a salon owner, where I remained in business, successfully for 11 years. By the time I was 28, my husband and I separated and then we divorced.

My clientele had grown, and I realized that so many people trusted me with all their hair and skincare needs. I was instrumental in helping people improve their self-esteem. When they left my salon, they felt better about themselves and they were ready to take on whatever, came their way with self-confidence.

I realized I was helping people in so many ways and in return I was helping myself. As time went on, I decided at the age of 31, that I was going to pursue a nursing degree. My experience in running my salon made it easy to multi-task, and the professionalism I maintained took me a long way in my present career. I had always wanted to be a nurse after all caring for people came naturally to me.

I became a Registered Nurse and I remarried, giving up my career as a hairstylist. To sum up my life, I would say I learned the importance of working hard and carrying myself in a professional way from my adopted grandmother and my late mother.

In the beginning, I felt like people did not understand who I was as a person and all their judgments and false accusations would often cause unnecessary anxiety, but because I focused on my daughter, I believe I am successful today. When I was at my lowest point, these are the things I did in spite of what I was going through.

1. I learned the importance of education, and why professionalism is a must regardless of what type of work, trade, or profession one pursues.

2. I learned to seek God and His Word not the negative words of others. I know who I am. I no longer seek validation from the wrong sources.

3. I made time to be by myself and meditate.

4. I accomplished this by meditating, learning to appreciate myself when others did not.

5. I sought God and learned that all you need is God's Love and God's approval in life.

6. Forgiveness- It was very hard to forgive my mother for not raising me the proper way. But I understood when I became an adult, she never had a family and grew up in an error where children were to be seen and not heard. I knew my mother loved me and did the best that she could and that is all I need to know and feel. I know God has welcomed her into paradise where there is no more sorrow or pain. God surrounds her soul with everlasting peace and love.

7. I visualized all that I was going to achieve.

8. I enjoyed taking care of my children.

9. I studied hard day and night.

10. I joined a Church and I prayed with faith reminding myself that the Holy Spirit resides in me.

Conclusion

I am thankful for my life and that I overcame seeking validation. I no longer look for the approval of others because I now know that my validation comes from within. I did it and so can you. Be who you are and love the person you have become.

FINANCIAL EMPOWERMENT

"My mother told me to be a lady. And for her,
that meant be your own person, be independent."

(Ruth Bader Ginsburg)

The Making
of a Wealthy Woman

Alison Brown

Have you ever had a confrontation with yourself? You knew in your bones that **you** were meant for more? Maybe you have heard it called a, *"come to Jesus moment?"* This is part of my story. Part of what made me who I am today. Financial literacy for women, more specifically, wealth empowerment, is the single most important type of education women can pursue. It provides freedom. It provides choices. It provides power.

You may be wondering what put the "bee in my bonnet" to figure out money? Great question. I have memories from my childhood that center around money. For whatever reason, this has always been important to me. And having "enough" money is important to me.

Below is the journey of how I went from a paycheck-to-paycheck upbringing and mentality to a wealth empowerment coach and real estate investor. Keep reading to see how you too can go from feelings of "never enough" to a life lived in a creative and abundant mode.

Money & Women

Money is a neutral tool. And as with any tool the power is in the hands of the tool's operator. If a person uses a shovel to do something bad, we don't think the shovel is evil. It was a neutral tool. The same can be said for money. It is not bad or good. It is how you use it that matters. If women do not know how to use the tool of money how will we ever accomplish all the good, we were meant for?

In my research, I found this statistic particularly telling about women's financial literacy in today's world. *"Women live paycheck to paycheck roughly 5 times as often as men. Of the 43% of Americans who live paycheck to paycheck, 85% are women, according to a new poll from insurance and employee benefits provider MetLife of over 8,00 US Adults over the age of 18."*

The first step to creating real, generational, wealth is financial literacy. Unfortunately, financial literacy is not taught in schools. In this modern era, women should be able to maximize **both** their earning and investing potential. One Chinese proverb states, *"Tell me and I'll forget; show me and I may remember; involve me and I'll understand."* Women need to be active participants in their financial futures to get the most benefit.

My Upbringing

I was the 3rd child in my family. I grew up in southeastern Wisconsin. While my household was a two-income family, I have some memories of there not being enough money. Feelings of missing out before FOMO was even a thing. We were not poor, but we did not have an abundance, either. This is commonly called living paycheck-to-paycheck.

My parents worked in skilled professional jobs. I would classify us as middle class.

Money Drama at a Young Age

I have two distinct early money memories.

One is when I am about five years old and my two older siblings got to go somewhere, and I was told by my older brother I could not go because I did not have any money. I cried and found my dad. When I told him, I was always being left out because I didn't have any money, he laughed.

Looking back now, most likely, he laughed since it was probably an activity. I was too young to do and not him laughing at my distress. He did comfort me at the moment, but he did not expect a child of my age to have money. I did. Even then there was a part of me that knew money opened doors. If money was the thing that was going to keep me from being left behind, I wanted it. This memory stuck with me all this time. It shed light on some of my beliefs around money.

Early Lessons in Saving

Another early money memory I have is when my parents set up savings accounts for us kids at our local bank. I remember walking over by myself to deposit my money in there. I loved the little bank account register books they gave us to record our money and "watch" it grow.

We were not necessarily taught to save our money as a habit. I wanted to do this. I had a desire to save from early on. I liked the idea of saving and I liked the idea of having money. So, I did try to put some of my birthday or Christmas money into that savings account regularly.

I also remember when money got tight and it was a while until payday, sometimes my mom would take money from our savings to buy milk and bread or other essentials. This was kind of distressing, but I also understood that we needed to eat. I have no ill feelings over this but perhaps that is why I did not conquer the habit of saving until much later in life. If saving was just going to be depleted for essentials, what was the point?

Not having my own money or control over my own money is a deep-rooted childhood memory.

The Path to More

When I was 17, I applied to an out-of-state private college. And I was accepted! Oh, the joy! I remember feeling excited. Since I was homeschooled and had no guidance counselor, I had to navigate applying for financial aid primarily on my own.

The FAFSA came back stating that I would get zero dollars in aid. Even though at the time we were a single income family, with five children as dependents, on paper we still made too much. With no aid awarded, limited knowledge of scholarships, and no savings to speak of, college seemed out of my grasp.

Considering the hurdles, financial and otherwise, I decided to take a year off and work. I did not feel comfortable going into that much debt before I was more settled on my major and possible career path.

During this time, my mom and dad purchased a career assessment program for me to work through on the computer. Remember CD-ROM's? Yes, it was one of those. It was interesting and gave me some guidance. In my mind, I needed 100% clarity if I was going to go into that much debt.

Timing is Everything

My one year off turned into five years. I was now 23 and had worked a full-time retail management position for two years. I felt blessed by that opportunity to explore working in the "real" world. Ultimately, it helped me decide I needed to pursue a degree to have a career in something besides retail.

It was time to pursue higher education. It was time to get out of that small town and fulfill the dream of college. I was the first one of my siblings to go to a four-year college.

I again applied to that same college located in Southern California. There was something inside me that told me this was the place I needed to be. And I was accepted (again)! I thought this school was best for me because of the small class size and I was impressed by the business major department.

One Last Hurdle

Weeks before I was set to move and I had given notice to my employer, I again did not qualify for much financial aid and I was too late in applying for a work-study position. They were all gone.

My dad was counseling me to postpone and not go to school. He felt like we did not have many options. We got into a fight about it. I dug in my heels. I was incredibly determined that my future depended on me going. I had already given notice at my job and trained my replacement. This was happening. I refused to accept that I had come this far to say "no" again.

My dad ended up calling the financial aid department and they said my parents should try to apply for a PLUS loan. Since they were in some hard times of being underemployed, he did not think they could get a PLUS loan. But they did. And to this day I am incredibly grateful that my parents did this.

At the time, I remember wishing that someone would have taken better care of me. Part of me was frustrated that my future was not better prepared for. I remember wishing that our family heritage was less working-class and more I-have-a-college-fund-for-my-kids. Then I could go to school and learn without the stress of *how you are paying for this* hanging over me.

Blessings of a Nontraditional Timeline

Blessings can come in unexpected ways. The first blessing of going to college later was that I did not change majors. I chose Business Administration with an emphasis in Finance and Management and that is what I graduated with. I had time to learn about myself and what I enjoyed doing. I wanted a degree that could easily translate to a career that could help me pay back my loans.

Also, starting college at 23 means by my sophomore year the FAFSA only required my financial information. I was in school full-time and not earning much money, so I now qualified for more financial aid options. I got grants and loans with low-interest rates. I was also awarded a work-study position along with some academic scholarships. I would continue to be eligible for them if I kept my GPA up, so of course, I did. Money is a great motivator to study when you are footing the bill!

Additionally, I took my studies seriously. I saw college as an investment in myself and not a rite of passage. I did have fun in college, don't get me wrong. I still have some of the best friendships of my life from that time. I was primarily there to get a degree, learn as much as I could in the field of business, and graduate with practical skills for a better career path.

I felt strongly that I did not want regrets around money. I wanted to be financially literate. I did not want to live paycheck to paycheck and settle for only "making ends meet." I did not know it at the time, but I wanted an abundant life. A rich life.

My Transformation

I thought that getting a college degree would set me up for success. And it did, partially. But when it comes to financial literacy, and creating true wealth, this was only touched on in some finance courses, if at all. Most of my wealth education has happened independently after college. As Jim Rohn is credited with saying, *"Formal education will make you a living; self-education will make you a fortune."*

For years, I thought I was doing all the "right" things when it came to money. In 2018, I realized I had left my money mindset unexamined. I had some difficult memories around money and therefore some limiting beliefs to expose. When I started addressing the thoughts I had about money and building wealth alongside my husband that is when I saw the most impactful changes in my life.

When I went through my struggle with my money mindset at times it felt futile, but because I focused on myself, my husband and daughter, and the dream life we **both** wanted to build, I believe I am successful today.

Today I am a college graduate with a degree in Business Administration - Finance and Management who graduated Summa Cum Laude in 3.5 years. I am also student loan debt free! I graduated from a private 4-year college with only about $20,000 in student loans. These were paid off within seven years of graduation. I have also become a real estate investor alongside my husband, and we own $5 million in assets.

Even though I am now successful, three obstacles I had to overcome were a history of paycheck to paycheck living, a lack of personal initiative in building our wealth as a partnership, and a disconnect between being a good money manager (budgeter) and having a great money mindset (thoughts).

The framework I developed that helped me to achieve my transformation, and now I coach others on, is called the 7 Habits of a Wealthy Woman.

7 Habits of A Wealthy Woman

1. A wealthy woman invests. She trusts in her ability to have her money make more of itself.

2. A wealthy woman never stops seeking financial education. She is personally dedicated to this.

3. A wealthy woman gives back. She finds opportunities to give back that deeply resonate with her.

4. A wealthy woman practices self-care. This includes the physical, mental, and spiritual aspects of her life.

5. A wealthy woman is committed to thought work. She knows you cannot outsource the internal work.

6. A wealthy woman seeks to practice gratitude every day.

7. A wealthy woman is intentional in relationships. She knows the value of socializing with people who support, encourage, and inspire her.

Now, looking back at how I went from a paycheck-to-paycheck upbringing and mentality to a wealth empowerment coach and real estate investor I attribute my biggest change to a mindset shift. I needed to believe I was a wealthy woman, worthy of wealth before I could see it and achieve it!

This shift saved my life because it took me from numbness, settling, and a powerless money mentality to being empowered in my relationship with money. This has ultimately created a life of peace and freedom to fully experience an abundant life.

Leonhardt, M. (2019, October 14). Women live paycheck-to-paycheck roughly 5 times as often as men here's why. Retrieved August 19, 2020, from https://www.cnbc.com/2019/10/14/women-live-paycheck-to-paycheck-roughly-5-times-as-often-as-men.html

THE VALUE OF YOU

Chany G. Rosengarten

When you understand value, you won't need to sell your soul for money. If you're doing things you wish you wouldn't have to do to earn money or staying stuck in a place, job or relationship because lack of money keeps you chain-balled, I understand because I was there too. If you've been struggling for money or dreaming of that big break that will finally set you free, or if you've been seeing the lifestyle of others, how they enjoy the wealth you can only fantasize about, this story is my gift to you. I'm Chany Rosengarten, and I'm going to tell you how I went from poverty to having enough, and how you can too.

Money doesn't solve poverty, value does. Money can come to you. The chase can end. The desperation can ease up. And you can finally experience wealth.

Poverty is lacking sufficient money to live at a standard considered comfortable or normal in society. In the United States, 13.9 percent of people, or thirty-nine million, live in poverty. And poverty affects not only the wallet, the dinner table, and the type of shoes you wear. Poverty impacts relationships, parenting, health, education, ability to work, and mental health. With rising rates of unemployment comes individuals and families experiencing poverty. Today, understanding how to get out of poverty is more important than ever.

The Beginning of Brokenness

I grew up poor. Now, I appreciate that as a "poor" person in the United States, I was way richer than most of the world's population. I had a roof over my head, food in the closet, and clothes, too. Fancy clothes. But I felt poor. I was anxious about money since I remember myself. And I worked from the day I was ten.

My parents both eschewed money. My mother's parents had had a brief moment of financial comfort- at the same time that my grandmother became deathly ill. To my mother, wealth equaled fear, and loss. My father believed that living with less was a virtue. Both of them were held in the chokehold of poverty, always in financial crisis.

I was trying to save my parents and trying to give myself the things I knew I could never have. So, I worked as a nanny from as young as I could remember, and I watched and diapered children, folded mountains of laundry, and cooked large family meals. I was capable, and for five dollars an hour, I was willing.

I got married young, in an arranged marriage, to my husband who was a student at the time. The matchmaker negotiated a fair deal: I would work to support the family, and my husband would continue to study. The way my parents saw it when they agreed to the deal: for a good boy, you had to be willing to pay. The way I experienced it: I wasn't *worthy* of being loved, I had to work for it.

I got a job as a teacher, and my take-home pay for the month was six hundred dollars. Rent, meanwhile, was nine hundred and fifty. Our first month's rent, we paid with our wedding presents. The months after were pure struggle. Buying maternity clothing was out of the question. Making the rent was our only focus, as it was impossible. My husband took an evening job as well, after his studies, and I worked three side jobs, just to bring in another few dollars. Every minute we had was dedicated to surviving financially.

That same year, we had our first-born baby. We did not have money for clothing for him, and we received a crib and a carriage from our parents. I dressed him in hand me downs and cried as I closed the snaps, not being able to give anything to my baby. This child was followed by another.

Every morning, I'd tear myself out of a sleep riddled with his colicky newborn needs, bundle us both into coats, and drop him off at the sitter, before running to my job. My body was depleted, but we needed the money. I felt like a slave.

With two young children, we moved across the continent. Rent would be cheaper in the new, third world country, and we got a small financial incentive to move, so that was all it took to convince us. But finances were even harder there. After a year of living there, we had so little money that we didn't have enough for food.

Broken All the Way Down

I remember the day we no longer had any money. The food used up and the pantry was bare. The fridge and freezer still ran but there was nothing inside, save for a small clear plastic bag of rice the size of a fist. I didn't cook it.

During that time, my cousin was getting married, and my aunt invited me to come to the wedding. She offered to pay for half of my travel expenses. I hadn't seen my parents and siblings in over a year and I yearned to go. But I told her that I couldn't afford the other half of the travel expenses. I was trapped by my lack of funds.

That night, my husband and I took a walk up the hill. Walks were free.

We sat down on a bench and I cried. "I gave up on buying new clothing. I gave up on traveling to see my family. I gave up on eating anything more than home-cooked staples. But basic food? We don't even have vegetables or bread." I had gotten lower than I ever knew was possible.

Rent was due that day. It was evening already. We didn't know how to pay.

"Ask your aunt to help us. She had been willing to give you half of your traveling expenses, so clearly, she has the money. That would be just enough for rent, and then we could use whatever else comes in this month for food,"
my husband suggested.

"I can't possibly do that. She offered it because she wanted me to attend her daughter's wedding, but what choice do we have? If we don't have rent, we won't be able to use the money that we do earn, for food. It's either we eat, or we beg."

And so, scared as I was at the new low I was experiencing, where food was no longer an option, I swallowed all sense of sanity and self and called my aunt. She sounded hurt and told me she would discuss it with her husband.

I don't remember if she gave us the money and I don't remember how we paid the rent, but I do remember how it felt to betray myself.

We survived, but my ego was shattered. During that time, I also asked my three closest friends to help me. They all said no. I was cycling out of control and grabbing at straws. We had three children to feed, I was walking around with torn clothes, and I bought only what was absolutely necessary, approaching the checkout counter with a familiar, sinking feeling of dread. My marriage was taxed to the point where it felt like it would snap, and I felt unsupported, angry, and desperate.

Refusing Repair

One day, I got an anonymous envelope in my mail slot. In it were three hundred-dollar bills. I ran through all the possible people who may have stuffed it into my door but could not figure it out. I felt intense shame at living at the behest of other people, and yet I also knew that this money would be used, that there was no way I could refuse this mysterious gift.

That evening, when I put my kids to bed, I went into the bathroom and sat myself onto the closed toilet seat and cried my most desperate tears. I cried because I felt completely powerless, but I was also angry. I had done everything I knew, to get myself out of the grips of poverty. I worked hard. I was a good person. I was raising a young family while working full time. What had I not done to change the situation? And still, it was only getting worse and worse. I felt burning rage, mixed with my shame. There were so many millionaires in the world. I was so jealous and neglected. Why could they have so much when I had so little? What would it take for me to earn two thousand dollars, enough to live comfortably inside of my small, cheap life? Why couldn't I make enough just to cover my rent, food, and maybe a new shirt once a year?

Broken Spirit

I felt such deep shame. Who was my benefactor? If I had at least known who was the one who gave me the money, I could assuage my feeling of public humiliation. But now it felt like the entire world was privy to my failure. For all the work I had always done, this is what I had to show for it: less than nothing. I couldn't even earn enough to keep myself alive.

I felt anger. Was this the way now? Was my only way forward, living out of other people's palm? And what if they wouldn't be willing like my friends had politely declined to help? Where would I go next? Did I deserve any autonomy at all? Maybe all the things I suspected about myself, that I was unworthy and unlovable, that I was weird, and I didn't fit in, turns out it was true. Poverty was my proof.

I feverishly considered what else I could do to drum up cash, but I knew it was futile. All avenues I knew of, I had tried. I already worked every day, from when my children left the house, until they came back home, often stealing back to the computer if I could ignore them, and always pulling all-nighters to add hours and work, work, work. I was overworked, overwhelmed, and exhausted from trying. I knew I was stuck in the land of poverty, trapped with no emergency door.

"There has to be a better way,"
I heard myself cry through the soaked towel, "there's got to be a way."

I didn't know of any better way. All my life, I was stuck, stuck, stuck in poverty. All my life, hard work was the only thing I knew, that, if I slaved hard enough, I could rub a cent or two together and give it to the most pressing need. All my life, I knew of need, of desperation, of hunger: hunger for food, hunger for worthiness, hunger for joy, hunger to know I had enough. All my life, I felt neglected and overlooked, abandoned, and alone. I could dream, I could yearn and crave, but I could never have. I could work, work, work until my bones ached, but I could never reach the place of enoughness.

There had to be a better way, and I was about to find it.

Fixing the Broken Pieces

1. **Learning Finances**. The first thing I did was to gather information. I started reading ferociously on the topic of wealth. Reading opened up a whole new world for me. It wasn't anymore me vs. wealthy. It was all of us, empowering ourselves through financial literacy. I learned that I didn't have to yearn for wealth, I actually deserved to taste it, to own it, to be it. Information gave me confidence.

2. **Connection**. But information alone is not enough. Poverty is borne in isolation, and wealth is brought forth by connection. I needed to talk to people who understood what it was really like. Until that day, I had only spoken about my struggles, if I needed my close ones to save me. Now, money became my conversation. I found people who, just

like me, were climbing out of poverty and healing unworthiness. And I started being honest about what it was like.

3. **Mentoring.** The most important thing I did was get mentored. I had experienced so much shame about not having. From the first time I intuited that my parents didn't have enough, I internalized the shame. I worked and worked but it never helped. There is never enough money to heal inadequacy. I needed to talk my shame out, I needed for it to be held and healed. My mentor did that with me.

4. **Faith.** What I came to, was trust. I remember the first time it occurred to me that if working wasn't the answer, I could ease up on the work and trust that money, which is an abundant and ever-flowing resource, would find *me*. It was difficult to let go of constantly trying to control. But I did. The day I finally let go, I got a job offer that was easier and more lucrative than any I had ever had before.

5. **Dignity.** Finally, I learned how to honor myself by saying no. For more than twenty years, my problem was money, and my solution was work. Work, no matter if you can. Work with a tiny, colicky baby. Work when my bones ached. For the first time, I learned to listen to myself. I heard my desperation. I heard how uncomfortable a job offer was for me. And I learned to say no. Saying no was a yes to myself. Saying no was a yes to my trust. Saying no was yes to money in a dignified, easy, simple way. Saying no was welcoming in wealth.

True Meaning of Wholeness

My story is one of valuing myself. Because what is money really if not the worth and value of things. How much is that vacation worth to you? How much is your time worth to you? How much are *you* worth to you?

When we value ourselves, we are saying, "Sweety, you are worth it. You are *so* worthy." The money follows like a manifestation of a dream.

If you are stuck in the poverty cycle, then you are not alone. Millions of women are with you and rooting for you. Poverty does not define you. I got out of poverty, even though I was married, with three young children, no education, and coming from the poorest municipality in the state of New York, where the poverty rate is seventy percent.

I did it by valuing myself.

My story is not a get-rich-quick thing. Believe me, in the years when I did everything for money, I tried those, too. They didn't work because inside of me was an unworthiness so deep, I was like a clogged pipeline. I believed my shame, I believed my unworthiness, I believed my poverty, more than I trusted money to find me.

But the more I invested in myself, my stocks grew. My stake in myself grew. And the dividends are infinite. The one investment you can never lose is the value of yourself, because you are inherently, infinitely, worthy.

When I was stuck in poverty, I dreamed of a six-figure income, a home with a manicured garden, a vacation to Miami. It was a fantasy I knew I could never have. All those things came, not by relentlessly pursuing it. It came because I relentlessly pursued *me*.

Freeing myself to be who I am, I finally become worthy and ready to receive.

You don't need to work harder. You need to love yourself more.

Sexual Abuse
Survivors Empowerment

"We must send a message across the world that there is no disgrace in being a survivor of sexual violence – the shame is on the aggressor."

(**Angelina Jolie**)

IT'S OK NOT TO BE OK

Lisa Campbell

Revealing your truest self by taking off your mask is not for the faint of heart. It takes courage, it takes strength to fight the battles no one sees, the battles that keep you suffering in silence. It's hard to break the façade that you created in order to feel protected. Until you give yourself the promise to be ok with not being ok, you will not be free.

I chose to take off my mask and allow myself the space and grace to heal my trauma of childhood sexual abuse. Freeing myself of the pain of suicidal thoughts, depression, and anxiety; giving the little girl inside of me the voice she never had. Setting the little girl inside of me free from shame, guilt, worthlessness, and being unprotected. I would like to take you on my personal journey of how I set myself free and began to heal.

Sexual Abuse

Child sexual abuse includes a wide range of sexual behaviors that take place between a child and an older child or adult. These sexual behaviors are intended to erotically arouse the older person, generally without consideration for the reactions or choices of the child and without consideration for the effects of the behavior on the child.

According to childtrauma.org, one out of three females in the U.S., and one out of five males, have been victims of sexual abuse before age 18. And according to the American Academy of Experts in Traumatic Stress (AAETS), 30% of all male children are molested in some way, compared to 40% of females.

Childhood sexual abuse has been correlated with higher levels of depression, guilt, shame, self-blame, eating disorders, somatic concerns, anxiety, dissociative patterns, repression, denial, sexual problems, and relationship problems.

Depression has been found to be the most common long-term symptom among survivors. Survivors may have difficulty externalizing the abuse, thus thinking negatively about themselves (Hartman et al., 1987). After years of negative self-thoughts, survivors have feelings of worthlessness and avoid others because they believe they have nothing to offer (Long et al., 2006). Ratican (1992) describes the symptoms of child sexual abuse survivors' depression to be feeling down much of the time, having suicidal ideation, having disturbed sleeping patterns, and having disturbed eating patterns.

I am telling my story of the social and psychological pain that I went through as a child-to bring awareness. I want parents to know of the warning signs of children suffering from sexual abuse. I want to let the women suffering from remnants of sexual abuse to recognize when they can no longer handle it emotionally.

Perfect Beginnings

Looking from the outside in, I had a perfect life, my parents were entrepreneurs, they built a successful restaurant and catering business that is still going strong today. 48 years later. They came from nothing and worked so hard to give me the life they never had, and they did that. I grew up in a beautiful home in Long Island, New York on the water. I am the youngest of five, but the age gap was so wide that I grew up as the only child in the household. My parents gave me everything financially. I never wanted for anything. All my cousins envied me because I always had the newest of everything, you name it I had it. I never flaunted or bragged about what I had because my parents made sure to instill in me that all of this comes from hard work, sacrifice, and dedication. My parents showed me at an early age the importance of dreaming big and that there isn't anything I couldn't do or be if I worked hard and put my mind to it. My life didn't come with financial struggles, but there were struggles, nonetheless.

In the first grade I was told that I had a learning disability. At that time, I was going to Catholic school and they told my parents I would have to leave school at the end of the year and attend a public school because they didn't have the right tools to help me. As a child I would try my hardest but reading and writing never came easy to me. I wanted to know what was wrong with me, why I wasn't as smart as the other kids in my class, I never got an answer to what the disability truly was. My parents were building a business working around the clock, they did their best to get me the help I needed however it was still a struggle. I would hate when the teacher would call on me to read out loud. I wanted to run out of the classroom, kids used to make fun of me when it was my turn to read. However, I always kept in mind what my parents instilled in me that I could be and do anything and that kept me pushing and trying to become better.

The Facade

As my parent's business grew, their hours at the store became crazier. So, they begin to rely on family and close friends to pitch in with watching me. At the age of six I was independent, I was making my breakfast, helping out around the house and helping at the store. My mom said I was like a little old lady like I had been here before. I had a protective nature of my parents and anyone I loved. I was compassionate and caring, I always wanted to make things better for others or worried if others were ok. I got that part of being protective from my dad, he was so loving, but he didn't play any games when it came to his family, let's say he could have been a professional boxer. I was a daddy's girl and he would always teach me the value of being grateful, meditating, and staying humble. He had a bigger than life personality, charismatic, and so funny he was loved by everyone that knew him. I was so grateful to have such a strong and loving father.

My mom was my best friend, even though she would come home so tired from her day. She would still make time for me and I loved that about her, she was a strong woman, very loving and was so giving of herself she was always helping others. My mom always kept it real with me, she never hides anything from me. She used to talk to me as if I was her friend but in a motherly way; she would always say "in order to make it in this world you have to be strong, only the strong survive." My mom had seen a lot of things in her life and had been through some tough times; she wanted to prepare me for life's curve balls, she wanted me to be a fighter and not to give up. I became that. I was a fighter, a tough cookie, I learned that no matter what you have to keep pushing past the pain and hurt to rise above.

She would always tell me that I could tell her anything and I always did. I loved the time we would spend together. She was full of wisdom. I never wanted to leave her side. I felt safe being next to her. My parents tried their best to be present in my life, however it was hard running the business and trying to be a parent. The time we spent together meant so much to me because they didn't have much free time. I would spend a lot of my time with my aunts and friends of the family that my parents trust.

I remember my parents dropped me off at a family friend's house and I would often stay there overnight or even for the weekends, my parents trusted that I was fine every time they left me there and I was for the most part, there were other children there it was always fun being around other kids my age. The family friend was a single mother and a very close friend of my mother, and she had four children: two sons one of the sons was around my age and the other one was a lot older than me and she had two little girls. Needless to say, the house was full; her older son was physically abusive to his little brother. He was big in size and his brother was so much smaller than him. I hated when he would hit him; one time we got into a fight because I was trying to protect the younger brother. I wanted to save him from getting beat up, me having this natural protective instinct I would jump into action without thinking. I didn't care that he was bigger and stronger than me.

I wanted to help my friend who was like a little brother to me; It was so hard to watch this and their mother would never do anything to stop it. She would say things like that's how boys play. It was so much more than that; one time he pushed him headfirst into a wall and he was bleeding and had a big knot on his head. During the fight I jumped on the older brothers back, he flung me off, I fell back against the doorknob, and hurt my back. I went into his mother's room and told her what he did, and she did nothing. Their mother was too busy entertaining her new boyfriend. She could care less about what was going on down the hall; so, I felt it was up to me to protect and save my friend. I hated going over there because of the older brother.

The Day My Life Changed

One day, my parents told me that they were taking me over there for the weekend because they had to work late that weekend. I did not want to go that weekend because I had got into a fight with the older brother the weekend before. I told my mom I didn't want to go. I wanted to stay home. She said, "We don't have anyone else that could watch you," and they would be leaving the store late. That meant I had no choice but to go, I packed my bag and off we went. When my parents pulled up to the house, something in my gut felt off and my stomach began to hurt. As I walked into the house, all the kids were playing, and I began to relax. I said to myself, "OK, this isn't so bad, the older brother was acting nice but as the night went on, the older brother started picking on his brother and I went off on him. He turned and looked at me.

The look in his eyes was one I had never seen before. It shook me to my core. Something shifted in him, he grabbed me, took me to the bathroom, closed the door and pushed me down. I fell on the floor. He got on top of me, held me down and pushed himself inside of me. I was trying to push him off, but he was too heavy for my little six-year-old self to move him. I could hear his little brother banging at the door. In that moment of him raping me, I felt my soul leave my body. I was powerless. The tears were rolling down my face. I felt lifeless. I tried so hard to stop it, but he was so much stronger than me. When he was finally done with me, he stood up and pulled up his pants. As I laid on the bathroom floor, he said that's what you get for trying to protect my brother. My whole life changed in that moment.

Powerless

When he opened the bathroom door, I got up, pulled my pants up and walked out as if nothing happened. His brother ran up to me and asked me, what happened in there? I had no words. I couldn't speak that whole night. I was in so much physical pain. What happened? I couldn't understand. I was in shock. I wanted my mom to come and get me. I felt so ashamed. How could I let this happen to me? I was so sick to my stomach; I couldn't do anything but just cry. It was the longest weekend of my six-year-old life because he raped me that entire weekend.

By the time my parents came to get me I was so drained, my mom asked how your weekend? I hugged her and said nothing. I wanted to tell her she was my best friend; but the fear of what she may think of me and the shame I felt for letting this happen kept me in silence. He was the first person to abuse me, but he wasn't the last. I was sexually abused until the age of nine.

As time went on, I became sad all the time, it was hard for me to sleep. I always felt sick. I couldn't shake what happened to me. I would act as if I was ok but deep down inside, I was hurting. I would pray to God every day to please take my life, the weight of this pain was so overwhelming. I hated myself, I would never sleep well because I would have nightmares about being raped. I would say why God why God. I never told anyone because I was so scared, and I didn't think anyone would help me. I used to get sad, withdrawn and angry. My parents would say why are you so moody you have everything in the world to be happy about, in their eyes they were right because they didn't know what I was carrying. They didn't know I had been raped multiple times even in my own home, they didn't know I wanted to take my life because of what happened, they didn't know. I so badly wanted to say something, but the fear kept me silent, the fear of my abusers and the fear of what my parents would think of me.

I carried this pain until adulthood. As an adult, I suffered from severe anxiety, depression, low self-esteem, suicidal thoughts, worthlessness, and insomnia. No one ever realized I was suffering because I was so good at wearing the mask "that I'm ok" people believed me. Until one day it all came crashing down on me. In 2002, I saw the older brother that raped me. I was with my mom in the store and he spoke to her and he said hello to me as if nothing ever happened. I froze for a second. This rage came over me and I cursed him out, my mom was so confused, and he said nothing only laughed and walked out. Later on, that night I couldn't shake seeing him, all of these feelings came over me and I couldn't stop crying. Something in my mind had shifted. I felt off, I felt unstable and overwhelmed.

Taking My Power Back

The next day, the feelings had gotten worse and I went to my mom crying and said I'm not ok. Something is wrong mentally with me. She couldn't understand why, what I did next changed my life forever. I drove myself to South Oaks, which was a mental institution in Long Island, I knew of it because I had often driven by it. I went inside and said I'm not ok, I began to explain what I was feeling and what had happened at the age of six. They said I was suffering from PTSD and seeing my abuser was a trigger, they gave me a card to see a therapist that specializes in trauma. I called the next day and that started my journey of taking my power back. Driving to that hospital was the first time I had put my needs before anyone else's, it was me advocating for myself, it was knowing that I'm not ok and being ok with that. It was taking off my mask and getting real with myself. I had finally given my six-year-old self her voice.

Unbreakable

I went from wearing a mask of happiness to cover up suicidal thoughts stemming from childhood sexual abuse, to successfully unpacking the negative emotions and becoming a trauma coach to help women take their life back after sexual abuse. This is how I set myself free

1. I had to get real in order to heal, no more wearing a mask.

2. Seek therapy, not just any therapy, cognitive behavioral or DBT, works best for trauma.

3. Allow myself the grace and space to heal. Allowing myself to feel whatever I was feeling without judgement or trying to stop it.

4. Acceptance on what happened, understanding it wasn't your fault.

5. Forgiveness: Forgiveness of self, others that you may feel that didn't protect you and your abuser.

6. Rebuild. You must create a new mindset, new ways of thinking, and dealing with issues.

7. Putting yourself first, creating a self-care routine is a must.

8. Asking for what you need/ talk about your feelings, (You matter ask, for what you need)

9. Setting healthy boundaries

10. Living and speaking your truth.

Healing wasn't easy by far, however, it was the best decision I ever made. After something like this happens to you, you will never be "normal" again, but you can heal and create a life worth living. You are worth the hard work, you matter. It's your time to take back your power and break the emotional chains that have been holding down. Take off your mask and free yourself.

MOTHERHOOD UN-PLANNED:
NEW TEEN & NEW MOM

Martha King, RN, BSN

I became pregnant at 12-years-old and six weeks after I turned 13, I gave birth to a healthy beautiful baby girl via emergency c-section. My pregnancy was not my fault, but I still felt ashamed and afraid due to the mistreatment of outside people saying that I would be on welfare, have a house full of children and not make anything of myself. Although I struggled as a teen mom, I still raised my daughter, finished high school, and fulfilled my goal of becoming a Registered Nurse.

By telling my story, I want to encourage teenage mothers to not only continue their education, but also get an advanced education, focus on raising their child or children, and avoid future unplanned pregnancies. I also want to help the mothers of teenage girls by revealing the low self-esteem and pain I felt as a teen mom in order to encourage the mothers to provide support, guidance, and education to their teenage daughters.

Adolescent Pregnancy

Teenagers from low-income families, rent-controlled subdivisions, and broken homes are more likely to be drugs and alcohol addicted, high school dropouts, and homeless; Latino and Black youth appear to be the most impacted.

According to statistics in 2017, from ages 15-19, Latino adolescent girls birth rate was 28.9%. Black adolescent females birth rates were 27.6%, and White adolescent females were 13.4%. Most problematic, only 40% of teenage mothers finish high school, and fewer than 2% finish college by the age of 30. In addition, 1 in 5 teen moms give birth again before age 20.

Teenage mothers should never give up on life because they are still a part of the human race. By educating our children, spending time with them, and supporting them, I believe that multiple teen pregnancy can be eliminated, teenage pregnancy can be decreased, and higher education can be increased. Come with me on my journey from childhood to grandmotherhood, so that you can understand how a pregnant 7th grader, with a lack of guidance, became a successful grandmother.

The Bastard Childhood

My mother moved to New York from Georgia when she was six months pregnant with me. She had two other children before me, bu t they were left in Georgia with family. One year after I was born, my mother had another daughter. One year after that, she met a man, got married, and had two more daughters. Consequently, I was raised to be the responsible one because I was the oldest of the second set of children, all born in New York.

Although I never met my real father, I was able to talk to him on the phone three times. He lived in Georgia, but when my mother would send me there every summer, my grandmother would not allow me to see him although he was only five minutes away. One time I asked my grandmother if I could see my father, and she yelled at me and said, "No, these people don't know you down here and you are ugly and black like him." I used to think my maternal grandmother hated me because I was born a bastard and dark skin tone. I said to myself, when I get older, I will come find my dad and my other grandmother. However, my wish did not come true.

Months after I turned 16, I got a phone call from my other grandmother. She was so nice to me and I didn't know who she was. I said who is this, she said this is your grandmother. She said, "Baby girl your daddy is dead." This was one of the worst days of my life. My heart was broken, and I wasn't allowed to go to the funeral. To make it even worse, my name wasn't written in the obituary. I then felt like the bastard child that my maternal grandmother viewed me as.

My Youth

Early on, my three sisters, my mom, and stepfather and I lived in a small apartment. There were only two bedrooms, a small kitchen, and one bathroom. One bedroom was for my parents and one was for us, four girls. Our bedroom had two sets of bunk beds. We didn't have a family room to sit in, so we played on the floor. There were six of us in this apartment until after I had my baby, which made seven.

We lived in a bad neighborhood behind a bar with a lot of excitement, but it was like being in jail. I was always the oldest in the house because we hardly saw our parents. My mother left me in charge of everything and we were all under 13. Every weekend, my stepdad would start drinking on Friday night and it would last until Sunday morning. I hated the weekends because we were closed in one room while the kitchen was full of drinking and what appeared to look like fun. I did not feel good about my life at all.

Youth to Motherhood

I was in the 7th grade when I became a mom. You are probably wondering why a 7th grader had a baby. Therefore, let me explain my road to motherhood.

My mom left us and my stepfather when I was 11-years-old. I was the oldest in the apartment with no guidance or support because my stepfather would come and go. One Saturday night at the age of 11, I was raped by my stepfather, also the only man I knew as a father. When it first happened, I was in the bathtub. He took me out of the tub and carried me to his room. This pattern lasted up until I became pregnant at 12-years-old.

Six months into my pregnancy I became sick, so I had to go into the hospital until I gave birth. I was on bed rest in the hospital for three months. While in the hospital, I used to sneak out of bed at night to go up to the children's floor and play ping pong ball and other games because I was a 12-year-old pregnant child that had no idea what was happening to me.

One evening I got out the bed, I fell, and I could not get up. The nurses found me during their rounds, and I was placed back in bed and wheeled to the nurse's station so I could be closely monitored. The next thing I knew, is that I had an emergency C Section the next morning and a 6 lbs and 10 oz little girl was born.

After I had my baby, my mother moved back into the apartment to take care of her because she said I was a baby with a baby. I was told to be a teenager and I had to go back to school. My mom told me even though I had a baby at a young age, I was still going to grow up to be successful and my baby was also. My mother was right, although other people said the opposite about me. I think my mother took better care of my baby than she did her own children because of guilt. However, my job was to finish the 7th grade.

The Great 8th Grade

While living in the cramped apartment with my three sisters, my parents, and my baby, I would sit on the bed and pray for better for my life, my baby's life, and my sister's life. Shortly after I turned 14, new owners took over the building where we lived, and they told my mother she had to move because there were too many people in the apartment. I was happy because my prayers were answered. However, we didn't have anywhere to go. My siblings went to their fathers' side of the family, and the born out of wedlock child was left behind on a mattress on the floor with a 13-month-old baby.

Before my parents found another place, one of my mother's cousins had an extra room so I moved there in October of 1979. I started eighth grade there and by the time my mother got to settle in her new place, my mother's cousin told my mother to leave me there until the end of the school year. I was 14 and this was one of the happiest times of my life.

Early Adolescent Depression

I was very sad and depressed because I was robbed of my safety and childhood. I was never the same after the rape. I used to be an active and outgoing kid that loved to smile, swim, handball, kickball, volleyball, track, and glee club, but it was all taken from me. My sadness was in silence because I was so ashamed and lost. I blamed myself for not telling, but I didn't know what to do. I thought it would all go away.

When I went back to school after becoming a mom, the other students were cruel, saying I heard you had a baby by your father. That made me angry because people looked down on me and I was labeled. I was scarred for the rest of my life by a man I hated until he passed away because I thought he ruined my life; I am still ashamed to this day.

I was judged harshly and ridiculed. Some of my friends' parents didn't want their children around me because I was a bad influence because they were unaware of what happened. Some of their children were a bad influence on me. However, I had a few friends whose parents didn't judge me.

On the contrary, some people looked at me with pity. I don't like people feeling sorry for me and I never played the victim even though I was. I struggled with my self-esteem because I was so ashamed of having a baby and I was a baby myself. After all of the sexual abuse, it put a lot of fear in me; I was always on guard thinking the worst of everything and everyone. I feared men because I thought they were all monsters like my step farther.

Mid-Adolescent Rage

The older I got, the angrier I became. I think this happened to me because my stepfather was getting back at my mother because he could not control her. It was all about power and control. He was a monster who made me feel powerless. There was no justice for me, and it was all kept "hush-hush." I blame both people who were supposed to be my parents. I figured out at the age of five that if you can't depend on your parents, then you can't depend on anyone. My parents brought me into this cruel world. I was an innocent child who was destroyed by the ones who were supposed to be taking care of me.

Although I had to still see the monster because he still lived with us, I was grateful to have help after the damage was done. My mother and my younger siblings helped with raising my daughter. Me, my sisters, and my daughter all grew up together.

Joys of Adulting

After I finished high school, I started working full-time and going to Nassau Community College at night. One day on a Thursday evening, my car broke down. I was with my 11-year-old daughter and her best friend. I had no idea what to do, so I sat there. A gentleman stopped, introduced himself, and asked me if I needed any help. I said yes. He said I know a good mechanic and I will go and see if he's available. He came back with this man. I asked his name and if he could please help me. He lifted the hood of the car, and twenty minutes later, my car was running. He said to me when you get home tell your husband I did this. I said I don't have a husband. He said I am right behind you...he has been behind me ever since.

We married after five years of dating. After we married, I went back to school and got my LPN with his support. I was able to go to school full-time and work part-time. After I finished my LPN program I was so happy. He said don't stop, go get your RN because that's what you want. I finished school and became an RN; I am in a good position in my life and I am thankful.

Overcoming Childhood Trauma

With the help of Jesus Christ, I managed to survive and grow up to be a successful adult. Although I struggle with PTSD, I am still blessed, and I am proud of the woman I have become. I got an education, my daughter got an advanced education, and then I got an advanced education. I also took care of my daughter until she got married. Although I didn't want more children, I adopted my late sister's infant son who is seven-years-old. I laugh and say, "I was too young with the first one and too old with the 2nd one."

These are the things I would tell any teens who are struggling with the things I dealt with.

1. **Responsibility**: I continued taking care of my daughter to make sure she has a better life than me.

2. **Mindset & Determination**: I refused to have any more children as a teenager without being married.

3. **Hard Work**: I made sure I kept a job. I always had a job from the age of 14 until today.

4. **Marriage**: I married a good man, who helped raise my daughter. We built a good life together. My husband helped me grow.

5. **Therapy**: I will be in therapy for the rest of my life. Therapy is an important part of my life. Therapy helps with dealing with the pain that I have been carrying most of my life. I try to stay positive, and drama free, no negativity.

6. **Goals & Dreams:** My biggest tool behind my success is never giving up on my dreams, working hard for what I want, and continuing my education helped make me successful.

7. **Prayer**: Pray yes, I will always pray and keep the faith. God has been good to me.

8. **Never Give Up:** I learned to never give up, no matter how hard things get, I also learned to not let what other people think of me bother me.

9. **Education:** I finished high school and college. Knowledge is power. My mom and sisters helped me take care of my daughter; we all grew up together.

10. **Confidence**: I learned to walk with pride with my head held up high because I am blessed. I stayed to myself and although I was hurting, I was independent and strong.

Grand-Motherhood

In conclusion, I hope my story helps teen moms and all moms to play a part in their children's success. From being a new teen and a new mom, I came a long way. The struggle was real, but most of my pain and misery has subsided. In addition to my husband of 25 years, my daughter, and my son, I am blessed with two amazing grandsons.

My grandsons have the complete opposite situation than I had as a kid. I lived in NY and went to GA every summer enduring the emotional abuse from my grandmother. However, my grandsons live in Georgia and they come to NY every summer so that I can take them on many fun adventures. Life has a funny way of turning out. The best thing to do is to keep going because the hard times will turn into great times.

ABOUT THE AUTHORS
Ayanna Mills Gallow, M.B.A.

Ayanna Mills Gallow, M.B.A, Visionary Author, is a Literary Strategist that maximizes success. Demonstratively known as a production leader and strategic marketer in the corporate world, she now has the same reputation in the publishing industry, as she applies key principles to have an unmatched proven track record.

Ayanna is also an Evangelist and a #1 Best Selling Author of Non-fiction Transformational books. As a first-year author, she wrote and compiled 10 bestselling books in 10 months. Ayanna's books are not only bestselling in the United States, where she lives, but also in the United Kingdom, Canada, France, Europe, and India. Recently, Ayanna's breakout novel, *God & Hip Hop: 21 Day Biblical Devotional Inspired by Hip Hop*, landed on the charts in Italy and Brazil.

Ayanna is the CEO of Thanx-A-Mills, LLC, a company she developed for book publishing and self-publishing consultations. Ayanna uses her strong literary skills as a facilitator at Authors Millionaire Mindset where she teaches students to achieve immediate results. Ayanna can be found at https://thanxamills.com/ and ceo@thanxamills.com.

Alison Brown

Alison Brown is a wealth empowerment coach and real estate investor as well as a controller for a civil engineering firm. Her coaching helps women go from abdicating their financial decisions to actively participating in building the life of their dreams.

For 20 years, she has been a personal student of money and wealth creation. Since 2015, she has semi-actively learned about real estate investing and how to create a portfolio of cash-producing assets alongside her husband. Then in 2019, she began ACTIVELY educating herself on how to create and manage cash flow positive investments through syndication.

Her passion is to help other women become empowered around money and wealth creation. She passionately believes that every woman should confidently be able to call herself a wealthy woman and truly believe it.

Raised in Wisconsin, Alison now lives in Nashville, TN with her husband and daughter.

Chany Rosengarten

Chany G. Rosengarten is a wife, mother of four young children, #1 Amazon bestselling author, and powerful motivational speaker. She teaches empowerment, self-care, and boundaries in business, love, and relationships, and her coaching, classes, and online courses have changed the trajectory of many lives.

As seen in the New York Times International Edition, USA Today, and featured on iHeartRadio, internationally acclaimed bestselling author Chany Rosengarten gives us easy-to-read, and compelling books on timely topics.

Charmaine Gentles

Charmaine V. Gentles, RN, MSN, ANP, DNP, RNFA is the first dedicated Nurse Practitioner for Long Island Quaternary Bariatric Surgery Program. Appointed to the position in 2005 to promote patient safety and improve patient care outcomes. Received her MSN and ANP from Adelphi University and DNP from Chamberlain College of Nursing. She is actively involved in promoting quality improvement strategies to improve patient health care outcomes.

Charmane West

Charmane West became a mother at the age of 15. She is now a registered nurse, with 21 years of nursing experience. She also has 20 years of experience as a cosmetologist, along with having owned and operated her own beauty business for 11 years. She currently works in a hospital where she attends to a variety of patients with different diagnoses including psychiatric illnesses.

Charmane is passionate about improving the lives of people, their health, and helping to improve self-esteem by encouraging and teaching clients on healthy approaches to caring for their mind, body, and soul. Charmane has eight Daisy awards for giving compassionate care. She was born in Harlem, New York, and is currently co-author of the new book *Saving Lives while Fighting for Mine*, Charmane lives in South Carolina. And plans to help people with improving their mental health, their self-esteem through writing, and giving motivational workshops online.

Jacinta Wolff

Jacinta Wolff is a registered nurse, who works in a cardiac step-down unit, mother, flutist, and writer. She mentors young nurses and loves being able to educate the public about their health and wellness through their sickness. When not at the hospital, she plays flute at her local church, plays for weddings and other events in the community. As a new writer, she is wanting to inspire women to find their identity, so they can be happy and fulfilled in their lives. She promotes self-care to women first so they can give their best to their families, friends, and community. Raised in Columbus, Ohio, Jacinta is the mother of four beautiful children Charlotte, Christine, Anthony, and Liam. Her children are all now out of the house and beginning to impact the world in their own way. She enjoys spending time with family and friends, nature, running half-marathons, being adventurous, and exploring new things. Jacinta has recently been honored with a Certification of Appreciation for outstanding performance and lasting contributions to the hospital she currently works. She was also given the DRC Impact Award with another employer, which states," At any time anyone can be the most important person in an organization." Next, she will be looking forward to teaching and uplifting more women to be able to find themselves and be confident in everything they pursue in life.

Dr. Keesha Karriem

Dr. Keesha Karriem was born in Chicago, Illinois. She is the Executive Director of a family-owned business that provides residential care to persons with intellectual disabilities. As a mother, aunt, entrepreneur, government worker, and college professor she is committed to instilling the values of truth and honesty. Dr. Karriem obtained her Doctorate Degree from the University of Phoenix and completed her dissertation on Stress and Emotional Intelligence (EI). Her analysis shows how EI contributes to significant life outcomes, such as better decision making and improved learning skills. EI helped her to cope and win again discrimination.

After recently becoming an aunt of two beautiful twin girls, she decided to create inspiring books that teach both young and old about Emotional Intelligence, diversity, values; and those with special needs.

To book webinars on Stress or EI or to pre-order your signed copy of the *Twins say Always Always Keep your Promises*. Please contact Dr. Karriem at dr.keesha@yahoo.com or on Twitter at Dr.K@Dr.Karriem

Lisa Campbell

Lisa Campbell is a successful Women's Empowerment and Trauma Coach. She empowers women to be the best version of themselves as well as helping women to take their power back after traumatic experiences. Her passion and love for helping others drove her to start a nonprofit organization and to volunteer as a patient advocate. Lisa's non-profit, Tuff Cookies, empowers, and mentors' young girls from the age of 8 to 18. In her role as a volunteer with The Safe Center in Nassau County, NY, Lisa served as an emergency room advocate for domestic violence and rape victims.

Lisa has been able to rise above all the obstacles thrown at her and has been a successful entrepreneur for the past 18 years; running two successful companies, mentoring, and supporting other entrepreneurs.

She was raised in Freeport, NY, and is the youngest of six. Currently living in Downtown Brooklyn with her fiancé and their two dogs. You can reach her, Lisa@taylormadecoaching.Com

Lisa Lamazzi

Lisa Lamazzi was born and raised in Chicago, Illinois. She is the Founder of Sexy After Divorce, a consulting firm that provides healing, completion, extreme self-love, and inspiration in getting men and women going through a divorce, ready to find true love. Prior to her current position, she was a Senior Account Executive and marketed for Doctor's for over 10 years. Lisa is a National Bikini Competitor and won 4th place in her first bikini competition. She earned several medals as a Spartan Girl and she also raised money for the Leukemia and Lymphoma Society and completed a couple full 26.2-mile marathons and ran one of them in memory of her Grandfather.

Lisa empowered/coached hundreds of men and women in personal development courses in various areas of life. She is still participating in this endeavor. She did all of this work as a volunteer. She is currently traveling the world, looking to attract her future husband, working from her computer, and will start to write her second book. Lisa can be found on Instagram and Facebook at Sexyafterdivorce and at sexyafterdivorce.com

Martha King

Martha Mills King, RN, BSN works as a Registered Nurse. Although Martha was forced to become a mother twice, her success and commitment as a mom is impeccable and her resilience is unmatched. Martha is an amazing mom to her 7-year-old son, Camron, birthed by her sister, and she is a devoted mom to her daughter, Ayanna, who was conceived in rape.

Since the age of five, Martha dreamed of becoming a nurse. After High School, she began her healthcare career and continued raising her daughter as a single mother until later marrying her husband, Louis S. King.

Martha triumphed over all trauma, which began when she became a new teenager and a new mom simultaneously. However, she embraced motherhood and life with the spirit of excellence and now she hopes to motivate other teen moms to do the same.

Tiffani Teachey

Tiffani Teachey is a Sr. Mechanical Engineer, Science, Technology, Engineering, Math (STEM) coach/advocate, professional speaker, and bestselling author of the children's book *What Can I Be? STEM Careers from A to Z*, and co-author of *Saving Lives while Fighting for Mine* anthology book.

As an engineer with more than 16 years of experience, Tiffani has a passion for inspiring the next generation to engage in STEM careers. She is known for motivating, empowering, and inspiring others to succeed. Tiffani was born and raised in Winston-Salem, North Carolina, enjoys traveling and being a youth mentor. For more about Tiffani, visit her website at www.tiffaniteachey.com, follow her on Instagram and Twitter @tiffaniteachey, or like Author Tiffani Teachey on Facebook.

TrevisMichelle

TrevisMichelle is a Registered Nurse who has pivoted to become an Empowerment Speaker assisting women, specifically Black Women, to take back their power, which may have been lost during or after a divorce. She graduated from Molloy College, and then went on to pursue a Masters, in Emergency and Disaster Management from Metropolitan College of NY. She has spent time in Israel, receiving a certificate from IMI Academy for Security, Anti-Terror Training on Emergency, and Crisis Management. TrevisMichelle has been recognized as an Influencer Within our Global Community "Women Hold Up the Sky" by the International Association of Women (IAW).

She is an active member of Chi Eta Phi Sorority, Inc., Theta Chi Chapter, a professional nursing sorority, upholding their motto, "Service to Humanity." TrevisMichelle is committed to ensuring that women SNAP out of the victim mindset so that they can live an emotionally healthy lifestyle. You can reach her on IG@trevismichelle or via e-mail info@trevismichelle.com.